Collins

CW00408852

Introducing English
to Young Children:
Reading and Writing

Opal Dunn

W

Collins

HarperCollins Publishers
77-85 Fulham Palace Road
Hammersmith
London W6 8JB

First edition 2014

10 9 8 7 6 5 4 3 2 1

© Opal Dunn 2014

ISBN 978-0-00-752254-5

Collins® is a registered trademark of
HarperCollins Publishers Limited

www.collinselt.com

A catalogue record of this book is
available from the British Library.

Printed in China by South China
Printing Co. Ltd

Cover images © Monkey Business
Images/Shutterstock; damircudi/
iStockphoto

If any copyright holders have been
omitted, please contact the Publisher
who will make the necessary
arrangements at the first opportunity.

Contents

About the author

Award-winning author Opal Dunn has many years of experience in teaching children aged up to 8 years, and has trained teachers all over the world. She has also authored picture books for nursery and young primary children, organised Bunko (mini-libraries) for bilingual, multilingual and double children (children growing up with two languages and two cultures) and has written information books and articles for parents. Opal is the co-founder of IATEFL YLT SIG (Young Learners & Teenagers Special Interest Group of the International Association of Teachers of English as a Foreign Language).

About this book

In the evolution of man spoken language preceded written language.

(Anon)

Introducing English to Young Children: Reading and Writing gives guidance for the transition period from pre-school English experiences to the more formal first years of written literacy in lower-primary education, up to the age of 8 or 9.

At this lower-primary age there are noticeable holistic and developmental changes, not only physical, but in attitude. Children start to feel they are more grown up. They want to be independent doers and learners. They are beginning to be aware of themselves and what they can do, and how, with effort, they can achieve and make progress. They need help to progress and to develop their own autonomy and we, as teachers, need to tune in to them and listen to their needs if they are to mature holistically and feel good.

For the child, English is still not a school subject; it's another way of communicating and talking within the class, school and beyond. Young children continue to pick up English in the same way as they learned their first language (L1), if the adult helping inserts the Playful Approach to motivate them. However, language content and enabling activities, although more advanced, are still linked to self-discovery.

The teacher's role remains important, as the teacher is still the main source of new input of English. However, teacher-talk has broadened to introduce a wider vocabulary through mediating and modelling situations. Direct teaching is now included in quick, focused tutor-talks that give explanations about language. Young children need help to develop their self-learning strategies if they are to become independent learners.

Young readers, who have developed their own multi-strategies to read, spell and write in LI, are impatient to do the same in English. Since they already understand the mechanics of reading, there is no need to teach them in the same way as non-reader English children. Readers only need help to find out how to transfer and reuse their existing reading strategies to read a new content. Once introduced to a multi-strategy approach to decoding English that they can speak, these children teach themselves to read. They have no need to start, like English-speaking non-readers, from the very beginning of the Synthetic Phonics Method.

Learning language continues to depend on the triangle (consisting of child, teacher and parent) for interactive support and motivation. Suggestions are made for how to involve parents' innate language-teaching skills in the home to consolidate children's learning. The window of opportunity to help children absorb English with enthusiasm is limited. By the age of 10, with the onset of puberty and the influence of peer-group pressures, their learning environment changes.

This book is about helping children acquire a good grounding in the basics of reading and writing English – and enjoying it. The many explanations and practical suggestions can be used to support a textbook or a teacher planning a school programme. What I have written is what I have observed, experienced and enjoyed with young children.

There is no substitute for caring human interaction and adult help for learning at this stage. However, as teachers we have to be aware of the increasing appeal of screens. To keep children's interest, we need to fire up and then stoke children's curiosity about the world in which they will need English.

Help me to do it myself.

(Montessori)

Opal Dunn —

List of figures

1

Acquiring language – The Playful Approach

1.1 Absorbing another language

A young child's ability to absorb language unconsciously, and seemingly effortlessly, is quite remarkable. It is even more astounding that the same young child, if given the right opportunities, can absorb two or three languages at more or less the same time, and use them with his or her different co-speakers correctly.

> *When I was 3 years old, I spoke three different languages to three different people. I am told I never mixed up the speakers. I just talked, but I didn't know I was speaking different languages until I was much older and my family told me. I can still speak these languages.*
>
> (Japanese lady, aged 45)

Young children, if circumstances are right for them, are innate, unconscious language learners. They are conscious of learning about the content of an activity, but not the language (or languages) they are using. At 5 or 6 years old they may tell you how many languages they speak and give examples, but they are not conscious of actually learning them in the way an adult is.

Children refine their language-learning strategies as they mature, depending on the type and quality of language support within their experiences. They then have the ability to reuse their language-learning strategies unconsciously, if motivated to learn another language – such as English. Most do this with confidence if they are shepherded by adults to take part in enabling activities, and are exposed to a similar quality of language support to that of their L1 acquisition.

By the age of 6, young children are familiar with most of the structures of their L1, although they are still absorbing new words and phrases. During pre-school children may have been introduced to different forms of spoken English or they may start an English programme during the first years of lower primary school. In all cases they innately expect to reuse their language-learning strategies to absorb spoken English through listening to it, as they take part in meaningful, playful activities. To young children learning language is not a task — it is not instructed, even if it is adult led. Young children have not yet developed the cognitive maturity to understand and use English taught as an abstract, grammar-based subject. Most of them cannot yet recognise the difference between a verb and a noun in their LI!

1.2 Transitions

Teaching methods in the first years of compulsory schooling depend on local society and cultural expectations. Parents and extended families often have culturally influenced opinions about how and when children should learn another language — in this case English.

Transitions (by which we mean the changes incurred by moving between schooling levels throughout compulsory education) alter the child's administrative status as a student. Transition is based on the child's date of birth rather than his or her level of maturity and readiness for change in methodological approach. There are few examples of free-flow schooling, where status and individual development are coordinated, making transition smoother for the child.

Transition from one school level to another generally entails an immediate adjustment to a more abstract style of learning, with teacher-led instruction and new expectations — even though there may be no change in the child's cognitive maturity, which continues to develop at its own rate following well-researched milestones.

The challenges in transitioning from home to pre-school are not likely to be great due to the close collaboration between family and pre-school staff. Both use similar supportive language patterns which are understood and expected by a young child. There is, however, in many societies, often a more marked difference between educational methods used in pre-school and those used in primary school (the first year of more formal compulsory education). This change is felt, if not verbalised, by the child in:

- teacher–child relationships
- types and use of language
- types of teacher instruction.

There is a new distance between the teacher and child, which young children feel. Gone are the many opportunities for caring, intimate, one-to-one dialogues with the teacher.

Although there may be a change in teaching style when a child enters primary school, teachers still have to focus on increasing the level of spoken English in preparation for the introduction of formal literacy, reading, spelling and writing. To do this successfully, teachers need to continue planning enabling activities in which children can use their existing language-learning strategies. Without these opportunities children find it difficult to pick up language to their full potential.

> *Parents virtualise start of normal school by uniform and a school bag. Play is seen as recreation and children are not sent to school to play.*
>
> (Stewart)

Transition to compulsory schooling is ritualised within many societies through material possessions like a uniform and a school bag, as well as in daily language within the extended family. Family discussions and expectations have changed to match the entry into formal schooling. Family members might say *You are going to big school now. Listen to what the teacher says. Put your hand up if you want to ask a question.*

Parents' comments about their young child's changed status are often influenced by their *own* school experience. Some parents support their children through transition by talking about their new English experiences with them in L1. Parents' understanding and mediation during transition to compulsory schooling is important as parents know, intimately, how their child learns as they have shepherded their language development since birth.

1.3 Play as a form of learning

Play is the highest form of learning and helps children to apply what they learn in an integrated way.

(Bruce)

Incorporating opportunities for play within new activities helps children become more confident, as well as leading them to become more divergent, reflective, inventive and persistent thinkers.

As the teacher's role is to provide a selection of enabling opportunities in which to acquire English, the atmosphere and teaching style in English lessons may be different from content-based lessons like Maths or Science. Some parents feel that since their children are now in compulsory education with a timetable divided into major subjects, instruction should now be more formal and should begin to resemble secondary school methods. Their reaction when their child refers to 'playing' in the English lesson can be of annoyance and they may openly criticise the teacher for not 'teaching', saying something like *I did not send my child to primary school to play! Play is for break time. I expect my child to learn English.*

'Play' is an umbrella term. In English the word *play* is broad and the meaning can be confusing. It can be used to talk about participating in a wide range of activities:

- *play football* (fixed rules and expectations)
- *play time* (free choice recreation at pre-school and primary school)
- *play 'Snakes and Ladders'* or *'Grandmother's Footsteps'* (culture-based children's games with a set of known rules)
- *play the piano* (the formalised learning of a musical instrument, following music rules)
- *play on a games console / tablet / smartphone*

The concept of play and its role in childhood differs from culture to culture; it can also differ between boys and girls. In some societies individual play is not valued as a way of learning, so some young children may not have developed skills to play by themselves and may wait for instructions from parents, teachers or other adults.

In a child's mind, the physical activity of play is like adults' work – children are intrinsically motivated to physically try out things, to find out how they work. However, to adults play can be seen as frivolous since it has no obvious aim, and in some cases has no adult presence.

Play is learning through doing: taking part in shared activities with a supportive adult or older child whose language the child can absorb unconsciously. A division between play and work only exists in the minds of adults who think in terms of formal teaching and instruction. For young children the two are blurred until the age of 5 or 6, when children begin to become aware of actually 'learning'. Any distinction made by children might arise from external symbols of a formal approach (such as sitting at a desk or using a textbook) but not from the *content* of an activity. Even if the content is more formal (such as a spelling test), playful use of voice and language by the teacher can make children feel that the experience is fun and they may even describe it to others as playing a game.

> *The main characteristic of play – whether of child or adult – is not its content but its mode. Play is an approach to action, not a form of activity.*
>
> (Bruner in Moyles)

A skilled teacher, like a young child's mother, regularly turns routine activities into what children think of as play, simply by using playful language. Furthermore, the playful nature of many language-learning activities is accentuated when contrasted with the more formal teacher-led instruction of other school subjects. This approach may account for the popularity of English teachers in primary schools.

1.4 The Playful Approach

To teach using the Playful Approach is demanding and tiring. The playfulness results in teacher–child bonding, but in a more mature and respectful way than in the pre-school years. This teacher–child relationship can contribute to the beginning of life-long attitudes to English, and such attitudes are formed early – before the age of 8 or 9. Later in life, adults often recall the name of their first English teacher.

The Playful Approach needs to be underpinned by:

- a hidden syllabus, influencing programme planning (including tutor-talk)
- assessments (short within the lesson, and longer after the lesson)
- flexibility (to respond to individual children's interests)
- knowledge about words and language
- modelling the use of new language and how to interact socially
- enthusiasm for discovery and learning language.

Language needs action as an accompaniment or the situation has no meaning for the children.

(Krashen)

Motivation is vital for all learning, whether it involves new or familiar content. Through the Playful Approach teachers can motivate and remotivate – although remotivation should be monitored as it can have a negative effect if overused.

Parents of very young children still learning L1 are skilled at inserting playfulness into regular activities to make each day's routine fun and motivating. Parents become adept at turning a routine like getting dressed into a simple game by inserting playful language, as well as using different voices and intonation to add surprise, wonder or suspense. Many parents say playful things like:

> *Does the sock go here?* [putting it on the child's hand]
> *No, no, silly me!*
> *You show me where it goes!*
> *That's right! Good!*
> *Where's the other sock? Here it is …*
> *How many socks are there? Two or three?*
> *Let's count …*

This approach, used innately by parents, must be transferred to English teaching so that young children can reuse their self-language-learning skills effectively to absorb the new language. The Playful Approach in class involves the use of playful language during an activity to turn it into a fun and interactive experience for boys and girls. Although playful language *relates* to the content, it does not alter the content or the content-related language.

The Playful Approach can be used when presenting new material and also when re-presenting material to be consolidated. In planning an activity, it is important to also plan the language that goes with it, including any accompanying playful language. Of course any plan needs to be flexible, adapting to children's reactions. Without planning language input, opportunities to extend language can be missed.

As the young child becomes more mature and lesson content becomes more structured, the degree of playfulness needed to motivate gradually decreases, limiting the use of the Playful Approach to the introduction of new material and routine remotivating activities.

1.4.1 Language techniques for the Playful Approach

✓ Language can be adapted to fit individuals, pairs, groups or a class.

✓ Language is supported by a hidden syllabus – a structured guide to increase acquisition. Teacher-talk can be flexible to follow children's interests and needs. Tutor-talks explaining new material need to be pre-prepared, so information can be focused and structured.

✓ Language motivates by inserting suspense, surprise, mystery. It remotivates, when focus has been lost, by extending short attention spans.

✓ Language arouses curiosity, inserts wonder, challenges 'how' – leading to critical thinking and creativity (for example, *Imagine if there was no sun? What if …?*).

✓ Language encourages effort (for example, *Try again, I know you can do it. That was good but next time let's do it better.*).

✓ Language challenges (for example, *If we have no electricity, what shall we do?*).

✓ Language encourages enthusiasm (for example, *Wow, that's great? I like that!*).

✓ Language supports exploring and discovery (for example, *Look at the size of this whale!*).

✓ Language inserts humour – play within play – arousing and creating it, and responding to it.

With regard to translations, these should typically only be given once so that children have to focus and listen carefully. Where possible, teachers need to develop children's gist understanding – a technique they are still developing in L1 to follow new ideas. Where further translation is needed, teachers often find that one child eagerly translates for other children. This means the teacher often has no need to revert to using LI. If there is no 'child translator' the teacher can repeat, supporting with more modelling. Children usually understand more than they can say.

1.4.2 The Playful Approach within games

Games sometimes lack speed but by including playful language English teachers can regain focus and momentum without changing the game content. For example, they could say *Whose turn is it now? Ok … who can find the ball?* The language teacher who includes playful language in games:

- creates suspense and excitement (for example, *Will I get a six? … YES!*)
- adds energy to speed up formal games (for example, *How many have you got? Oh, Toru can get more. Hurry, I'm next. No, sorry, it's your turn.*)
- focusses on both winners and losers (for example, *You did well. Next time I think you might win.*)
- creates an enjoyable game-like atmosphere (for example, *Oh, can you get a red one? Let's see …*)
- sums up progress regularly and predicts possible outcomes, sometimes incorrectly, to amuse (for example, *Now everyone has five cards. I know who is going to get six cards first. It's … !*).

Much of the content and ways of working in English games and activities may be unfamiliar to children, as culturally they may be quite different from LI games. However, at a later stage children like to prove their ownership of an activity or game by showing they can manage it by themselves and take control, even if the teacher has initiated play and set the scene. Adults need to respect this and patiently wait during the initial tries, whilst the child self-corrects through trial and error, rather than jumping in with the correct solution. Overt correction of game playing in front of others can dent children's pride and demotivate! Children need to reflect, reconsider and redo if they are to be creative.

Once children know how to play a game well, they often act as home-play tutors to their family when playing games in L1 or English. Much to the delight and amusement of parents, their children naturally insert the games at home.

1.4.3 Poor play experiences

Teachers need to continually observe, assess and record children's type and level of play and be ready to add guidance and add further challenge where needed. Where play is repetitive and at a low level of cognition, the teacher needs to get involved by sensitively interacting with new language or a relevant new object. This will stimulate interest and also scaffold a child's next level of cognition.

Where teachers are not sensitive to children's low-level satisfaction and achievement in an activity or game, children can lose interest and can easily become bored or frustrated, saying *I don't want to play. I don't like this*. Interest should always be restimulated before the end of the lesson, since a lack of volition can easily spread to attitudes at home and carry on to the next lesson. Loss of interest can also foster parents' belief that English lessons are nothing but play and that their child needs more formal instruction.

> *The art of a skilled teacher is getting the right balance, by providing structure whilst supporting autonomy.*
>
> (Stewart)

1.5 Free-choice time

Young children need repetition. Children, without adult help or intervention, repeat games or activities until they gain ownership and control over them. This can most easily be seen in the playground during break time where – either by themselves, in pairs or in a small group – children play the same game with the same rules over and over again. Children need opportunities to experience repetition like this in the English classroom and also at home if they are to gain ownership and control.

'Flow' is a state of complete immersion in an activity.

(Csikszentmihalyi)

'Free play' was valued by Froebel, Vygotsky, Montessori and Bruner. In the 1960s Bruce renamed it 'free-flow play', to include the work on 'flow' by the psychologist Csikszentmihalyi.

In 'flow' experiences:

- Children are totally in control and self-regulated.
- They are completely immersed and engaged in intense activity.
- Children's bodies and minds are stretched in a voluntary and possibly unconscious effort to achieve something.
- They are free from adult direction.
- They are confirming what they know and absorbing it more deeply.
- They gain self-satisfaction, confidence and an inner feeling of happiness.
- Their concentration is so deep and they are so engaged that they are not aware of themselves.
- Their involvement in the activity is unconscious, like breathing – they don't have to think about it.

'Flow' can often occur during activities or games and is associated with achievement and intrinsic self-satisfaction, giving confidence and a feeling of happiness. When it occurs and the length of time it lasts cannot be predicted – all teachers can do is 'set the scene' by programming time for free-choice activities. Flow experiences commonly occur in Montessori-type settings, when children are immersed in using game-like materials. Adults may not always notice (or may never have noticed) a child deep in a flow experience.

Consider the following description of how children might modify an activity once they are immersed in a flow experience:

> The teacher gives the children a complete set of pre-prepared word cards (such as *foot* and *ball*) which make up compound words (such as *football*). The children are asked to take turns putting word cards together to make compounds. The set might include:
>
> **foot ball snow man cup cake cow boy butter**
> **fly sun flower toe nail bed room black bird**
>
> After a while, the children decide to change the activity to a type of memory game, putting all the cards face down. They turn the cards over one at a time. Children have to keep all the cards in their hand if they can't make a compound word, or put one down if they can. The winner is the child with the most compound words.

The value of revisiting an activity or game for young children, free from adult direction, is often undervalued in classrooms. Free-flow experiences can include book browsing, which gives children an opportunity to revisit and reread a book independently, organising and controlling their relationship with the story. Through this self-regulated, fluid and adult-free experience, children are able to confirm what they know and absorb it more deeply.

Too much adult-led structure can stifle originality and the self-motivation needed to think and create. A class with only teacher-led activities which do not include the Playful Approach can stunt children's innate passion. As well as this, frequent chances to repeat activities are needed so that children have the opportunity to repeat patterns – which is crucial for learning.

> *Free-flow play is an integrating mechanism which brings together everything we learn, know, feel and understand.*
>
> (Bruce)

1.5.1 Planning free-choice activities

Time is limited in many English class programmes, but most teachers manage to fit in a free-choice period at least once a month (or if lessons are daily, once every two weeks). In some schools free choice takes up a major part of the lesson time, often taking place after the warm up, or after the summing up at the end of the lesson. In larger classes, children can be divided into two groups, one working with the teacher and the other enjoying free choice. The group changeover can take place within a single lesson, or in the next lesson.

Where teachers cannot fit a free-choice session into their programme, they can make opportunities for children to take activities home to help them revisit a game, book or other activity and experience a sense of flow.

> *Happiness depends, as nature shows,*
> *less on exterior things than most suppose.*
>
> (Anon)

Discussion about which free-choice activities will be available in the allocated lesson is an important part of the flow experience. In free-choice situations, children have the freedom to make their own choice from the activities on offer, including book browsing and games that they want to revisit. Teachers need to listen to children's requests as well as making their own suggestions and noticing children's reactions to them. This reflective preparation plays an important role for children.

Young children are used to self-regulating their play on screen. They are completely absorbed, returning again and again to the same video game without adult intervention or even sometimes understanding the accompanying language. They manipulate the game until they have mastered it and then happily move on to the next level or game without taking a break. This is another type of flow experience, which can set the level of children's expectations for off-screen activities.

> *'Flow' has been associated with increased performance in work, sport and in school.*
>
> (Stewart)

In free-choice activities children can:

- reflect and make choices (critical thinking)
- self-initiate
- self-motivate
- self-manage, working at their own pace
- concentrate, persist and remain focused
- consolidate their learning, taking it to a deeper level (metacognition skills)
- problem solve, discover and rearrange (creativity)
- collaborate with a partner or group members (social and emotional growth)
- work without interference, except for guidance and encouragement from the teacher when required
- work without external pressure (no fixed process) or set aims or goals (no end products)
- work without rules, except for usual classroom or game rules (no right or wrong, no need to conform to adult-imposed standards)
- harness emotions and find out how to manage them
- imagine and insert humour
- work on building self-learning strategies
- explore new paths
- experiment and take risks
- repeat activities as often as they like.

1.5.2 Managing free-choice activities

Arranging free-choice activity sessions within an English course helps to further holistic learning, since activities can take place in LI but are accompanied by a 'hidden' English syllabus. It also helps to further develop a positive mindset to learning English, as it helps children feel in control of their learning.

During free choice some children revert to using 'private talk', thinking aloud and giving a running commentary to themselves (but for all to hear) about their activity. Vygotsky believed this unconscious, private talk helps to develop thought and self-regulation. It can be in LI or English or a combination of both, entailing 'code-switching' to fit words from one language into the other where necessary. Private speech can reveal a lot about a child's inner thinking and level of understanding, and with maturity this external talk becomes internalised.

To organise a free-choice classroom session, the teacher has to present a selection of activities or games which the children are already familiar with, and then manage the children's individual choices from the selection on offer. The teacher can present two or three possible activities, depending on what he or she feels the class can manage. The children's choices should ideally be made in the previous session, with children signing up for their chosen activity. As places are limited for each activity, some children's first choice of activity may be full and they may have to make a second choice. The teacher may need to teach them to wait until the next free-choice session for their first-choice activity. For example, the teacher could say *Only four names, please. Write your name here. This list is full now. What is your second choice? You can have your first choice next time.*

This choosing process involves critical thinking and in the first instances teachers need to help children by modelling how to think through the decision-making process and how to make decisions. This discussion around selection helps to develop children's social and emotional intelligence, as well as showing children how to appreciate the feelings and choices of others. Initially, the teacher has to lead in the choosing of activities, gradually building up a mode of child participation. With maturity and experience, children begin to organise their choices amongst themselves while respecting the feelings of others.

Within a free-choice session, the role of the teacher changes from instructor to consultant, eventually giving guidance only where necessary. Children should be in control and any interference, except to remotivate, could intrude in the child's world of reflection as they relive their chosen experience at a deeper level. In flow moments the child is functioning at the highest levels: imaginatively, creatively, innovatively.

Where children have chosen to work in pairs or a small group, the teacher's role is to encourage collaboration as well as awareness of feelings and relationships, while children gradually become more aware of what they and their peers know (metacognition). Different skills and competences are introduced as each child revisits known activities, exploring, discovering, repeating and practising skills.

Children may discuss amongst themselves in English or in L1. The teacher is there to recast back in English where they have used L1, or to inject a phrase or some vocabulary in English which can blend in with the activity.

Teachers have to bear in mind that in free play the *process* is more important than the *product*. Teachers should not always be looking for some representation of the child's work (or visible outcome) as this could inhibit the child's present freedom and their future attitude to free-choice sessions. During free choice, children have a *real* reason to use English. Teachers can discreetly observe and assess where children need additional practice with handwriting and/or developing their usage of descriptive words (adjectives and adverbs).

> *In every job that must be done, there is an element of fun.*
> *You find the fun, and ... SNAP! ... the job's a game!*
>
> (Mary Poppins, from the Disney film)

2

Tuned-in teaching

2.1 Acquiring English

Teaching young children effectively is not only about having natural common sense, it is about making sure that one has the knowledge and skills to interest children in the world about them.

(Engel)

The more we learn about neuroscience, the clearer it becomes that the human brain now develops much sooner than we had believed. Early stimulation can be highly effective. The spread of technology means many more young children can be exposed to English, a language different from LI, at an earlier age.

Although the Internet includes some very useful support material, we need to realise that a lot of content on the Internet is privately published and therefore not necessarily rigorously edited – in some cases information may be incorrect or not suitable for young children. For example, on some sites about the analysis of the 44 sounds of English, /oo/ is sometimes portrayed as representing just one sound rather than two (as in *book* and *food*). Many children already know this, however, through playing with language rhyming sounds, story refrains and rhymes.

Today's young children may well have moved into the stage of being able to analyse and recognise patterns earlier than on Piaget's original scale (see Jean Piaget's theory of cognitive developmental stages). This may be as a result of visual and oral exposure, especially from screens, from an early age. Due to children's diverse home experiences, it is quite difficult for teachers to assess how these experiences have developed children's self-learning strategies for language learning in either LI or English.

2.2 Tuning in

In many primary schools learning language remains a different experience from learning a core-curricular subject like History. Learning language is still a shared activity – a dialogue between the child and the teacher, older children, parents and extended family. Vygotsky used the term 'social constructivism' to describe these moments when children and others who are more experienced make meaning together, by both concentrating on the context of an experience.

Without understanding the whole child it can be difficult to tune in to his or her needs. The English teacher needs to know something of the use of languages and the type of English-language interest in the child's home, in order to measure how much support and encouragement can be expected for homework (which in primary school becomes a regular additional consolidation activity).

Parents also need to understand the teaching methods and their role in homework. Without understanding the importance of the Playful Approach to provide motivation, homework can become a dreaded task. Without cooperation and helpful explanations, parents may find it difficult to tune in to their child's English lesson positively, or to understand the child's progress. Parents might compare the English lesson with the teacher-led instruction used in the other subject lessons.

2.2.1 Teacher–child relationships

By primary school a child's relationship with the English teacher has developed from that of a protective aunty-like figure in the pre-school years, to one of a caring teacher built on mutual respect. As primary-school pupils, children feel more grown up and more in control of themselves, ready to take responsibility. They now want to be independent and show they can make things happen, although they still need support and guidance from adults. Getting the balance right in the period between pre-school and upper primary is essential. The lower-primary years are an important bridge between the two, in which children need adult help to confidently develop over time their own self-learning strategies as they matures holistically. In helping the children, the teacher is not just thinking of teaching English, but also of adapting English input to the holistically-maturing children's needs.

Teachers are children's role models; they are the main source of the children's input, guiding and tutoring them whilst sharing with them spoken and written language to meet their self-learning strategies, needs and levels.

Young children still want to please their teacher and their parents, too. They look for their approval as it gives them confidence and assurance that they are doing the right thing. Young children want to feel successful, and can now measure their own ability, contrasting it quite accurately with others in their class. They generally know the 'ranking' of children in their class and teachers may hear comments like *Mari's the best at English. Akira knows a lot of English words about food.* Teachers often try to disguise group levels by calling them different animal names or colours, but children usually work out which is the top group! Children talk about who is the best openly amongst themselves and often explain it to their parents, too.

By lower primary most children are fluent L1 speakers and have been introduced to more formal L1 education (reading, writing, mathematics and science). At the same time they are still unconsciously absorbing more spoken English on which they base the acquisition of formal English literacy skills – reading, spelling and creative writing. Depending on the amount of exposure to English, many will have worked out how and when to use their personal language-learning strategies and unconsciously know which of their strategies are the most effective for them. Some may even be able to verbalise the way they like to learn.

If teachers themselves were introduced to English as an academic, grammar-based subject, they may feel inclined to introduce it to young children this way, too: through an abstract, grammar-analysis method with little chance for interaction or dialogue in spoken English. Although teacher-led instruction can often feel more fulfilling for the teacher (because progress is easier to observe and assess) teacher-imposed methods not involving interaction may not be as lasting or motivating for the child. Many young children also find imposed grammatical content difficult to understand, and thus absorb, as they have not yet been made aware of the grammar they are using naturally in LI.

Non-native-speaker adults need to be careful not to let how *they* were taught English influence their teaching or support methods, since young children need to self-acquire English using their finely tuned language-learning strategies. Research continues to confirm that language acquisition is linked to a form of physical self-discovery related to the cognitive maturity of the young child, whose brain is still developing. This seems to be the case in some situations throughout adult life, too. For example, many people find it easier to learn how to change a car tyre by watching someone who knows, rather than reading a manual!

2.2.2 The teacher's role

The teacher's main role is to enable the child to use and develop his or her self-acquisition language-learning strategies, whilst also allowing autonomy to grow. The teacher's role expands as the use of English becomes more advanced; they become involved in delegating responsibilities, organising more complex activities and in the introduction of formal literacy.

The teacher still remains the main source and model of spoken English. The teacher also now becomes responsible for the spoken and written English used in the introduction of formal English literacy skills. Through teacher-talk and tutor-talks, children have opportunities to absorb different styles of English and later to use the language. However, the child's acquisition of English is limited to the language the teacher uses and to the content of picture books. In lessons where teachers use only the textbook without talking around it or including extra activities, the child's acquisition is hindered by the low quality or quantity of input.

Textbook language plus some general management and game language is really not sufficient. Nor is it the right *type* of English input to enable the developing child to start talking about his or her interests or emotions, or to begin socialising and cooperating with other children. Children may need short periods of silence for self-reflection, but long periods of silence when there is no opportunity to listen and learn any English from the teacher (their main source of English input in the classroom) is a waste of children's learning time.

The use of different voices, intonation and language styles (descriptive, reported speech, etc.) is important as a teacher responds to changes within the classroom, or sees a need to remotivate. A sudden, whispered *Listen, children. Let's think about ...* can surprise and interest the class and quickly get their attention!

Once children have got used to picking up English, they appear to have refined how to use their self-language-learning strategies. Teachers should not underestimate children's ability to pick up English, and shouldn't let learning preconceptions limit the amount of input they given the children. Children are innate language learners and always understand much more than they can say. If they feel an overload they know how to switch off and wait to be remotivated.

> *The art of a skilled teacher is getting the right balance by providing structure whilst supporting autonomy.*
>
> (Stewart)

The teacher's main role is that of:

Motivator: using the Playful Approach to stimulate and restimulate positive interest in activities and formal literacy.

Modeller: using teacher-talk to aid understanding of emotional, social and classroom behaviour, as well as modelling new activities.

Mediator: introducing new challenges including tutor-talks to explain formal literacy.

Manager: planning lesson programmes, guided by the hidden syllabus and assessment but also following children's interests; indicating revision needs.

Monitor: assessing children within lessons and weekly to check progress and the need to revisit learning (this includes the summing-up sessions at the end of each lesson in which achievements and future plans are discussed).

Within all these categories there is more advanced use of language to ensure acquisition, formal literacy learning and progress in speaking.

Encircling all five roles described above are **Materials**, the base for enabling activities and formal literacy experiences. Many extra materials have to be collected by the teacher or sometimes, at the teacher's request, by the family.

2.3 The child's expectations of the teacher

A young child expects a teacher to be:

- friendly
- reliable
- caring
- full of enthusiasm and positivity
- a source of knowledge (or to know where to obtain information)
- an example of fair play in games (not accepting any form of cheating)
- just and fair in all personal comments and assessments
- respectful of any work in which effort and improvement has been made
- ready to co-share when a child or pair cannot manage alone.

The teacher–child relationship continues to evolve as the child develops and as the teacher gradually changes from leader to sharer or co-partner, using language and management routines in cooperation with the child until he or she is ready to lead alone. The degree of teacher support changes to match the child's progress, well-being (physical and emotional) and desire to do things autonomously. Within a single lesson language support can range from teacher-initiated and teacher-led, to shared-support, to child-led and child-initiated.

> **Teacher-initiated ⇨ Teacher-led**
> **Shared-support**
> **Child-led ⇨ Child-initiated**

Children have their own views on teachers and they openly tell parents who is their favourite teacher and why. Good relationships with the teacher and with their peers contribute to the intrinsic enjoyment that motivates children to learn English. A supportive relationship shows that the teacher values the children's ideas. It also encourages children to initiate sometimes, using phrases like *I have an idea. Can I tell you?* Children need to be confident that initiating is allowed in the English classroom, since, in some cultures, it's not always encouraged in L1 lessons.

It's also important to remember that children learn more from each other than from the teacher, as, from a child's point of view, peers are easier to copy than an adult.

> *Children learn strategies from watching each other, and are more likely to imitate what someone quite like themselves does rather than an adult.*

(Stewart)

Teachers need to constantly review:

- the changing teacher–child and teacher–class relationship and how it develops within the year
- how interesting they themselves seem to children – are they holistically 'switched on' to the children's world (including 'screen world')?
- how they present new content to children and develop their desired independence (autonomy)
- how they structure content to help make learning easier
- how they manage activities so that children have opportunities to work together and learn from each other (for example, with one child 'teaching' and peers learning)
- how they make children and families aware of progress.

The best motivation to learn a language is not an abstract liking of its beauty or utility, but a liking for the person who speaks it.

(Taeschner)

2.4 Enabling learning

... prepared input that alters according to the child's needs and interests.

(Whitehead)

Planning language input within a programme and lesson is paramount for progress. Thought has to be given to which language to reuse and where, as well as when and how to introduce new language. In addition, some language input needs to be structured very precisely so that children can absorb it easily and later use it themselves. However, 'planned language' also has to be adaptable to include impromptu language, as the teacher tunes in to the immediate interests and needs of the children during a lesson.

Children need quality, planned English input (and repetition of this input) if they are to pick up English to their full potential. This potential is often underestimated in comparison to that of children who learn languages outside the classroom effectively, rarely making mistakes. A child does not find learning language difficult like an adult; if he or she says it is difficult, it is generally a reflection of what adults have said!

Throughout the language learning process, the 'feel-good factor' is vital for motivation and new learning. Children live in the present and their well-being can change from lesson to lesson. Teachers need to tune in to their emotional state at the beginning of each lesson and adapt to it. Sometimes, if children are moving into a new developmental stage, teachers need to adapt quickly to satisfy their eager curiosity to absorb new information and ideas.

Focus (Attention) is a skill. Attention is embedded in well-being.

(Goleman)

Holistic learning for young children of 6 to 9 years is innate, rapid and continuous, following recognisable, common developmental patterns. By the age of 8 or 9 the child has matured considerably and has gradually begun to feel and portray his or her own identity. The child is more knowledgeable and can do more things alone, confidently repeating and consolidating known skills or discovering and trying out new ones. A child of this age is an unconscious self-educator and likes to be treated with patience and understanding.

2.4.1 Modelling language

Modelling the use of new language, or re-modelling known language and extending it to match new content, is important for learning. Acquiring language through structured modelling involves:

- teacher modelling (child watches and listens)
- co-share modelling (teacher and child work together)
- child modelling (leading the speaking, with teacher encouragement and support).

Modelling can be consolidated through playing quick games. Consider the example on page 41:

'Pass it on' game

Start the game 'Pass it on' by passing a packet or object to one child, saying *This is for you. Please take it.*

The child takes it and gives it to another child repeating *This is for you. Please take it.*

The other child takes it as quickly as possible and says *Oh! Thank you very much.*

He or she then goes up to anyone in the class and says *This is for you. Please take it.*

The new child takes it as quickly as possible and says *Oh! Thank you very much.*

He or she then goes up to anyone in the class and says *This is for you. Please take it.*

This continues until the teacher says *Stop.*

The child who has the packet when the teacher says *Stop* is out of the game for one minute.

To begin with, the teacher has to support each child as he or she speaks to make sure the English is correct, but once the game is known it can be played with two or three different packets being passed round the room at once!

2.4.2 The inclusion of enabling activities

Enabling activities need to be closely linked to assessment if teachers are to take children to the next level and work within the child's latest 'zone of proximal development' ('ZPD'). Vygotsky defined ZPD as the gap between what children can do on their own without help, and what they can achieve with assistance from an adult or more able peer.

Teachers must plan effective, structured enabling activities to match the developing child's need for new motivation and consolidation. Children have the ability to comment on their own work and are often aware of how well they and others have performed. Motivation plays an important role in achievement and to assess effectively teachers need to know how to react to growth and development of learners.

To achieve progressive learning, the teacher has to plan a programme which includes enabling activities as well as natural opportunities for repetition and reflective free play (or free-flow play). Teachers need to find ways to arouse curiosity in both girls and boys, whose interests can sometimes become markedly different as they mature.

2.4.3 The parents' role

Teachers have to be wary of how parents describe their children, particularly parents' perceptions of their children's qualities and faults. Sometimes parents may say, in front of their children, *She's very shy. He's not a good at studying.* Even though some children 'perform' in front of their parents, to please them, the teacher should not automatically accept the parents' description or the child's behaviour in this situation. Instead, teachers should find out for themselves – it could be that the child may want to act quite differently in the environment of the English lesson.

Although the lower-primary child is now more independent, the same basic triangle of influence and support (parent, teacher, child) remains important in English acquisition. New discoveries innately motivate children to try and express their thoughts, imagination and feelings with others in English. Discovering the world at this age is exciting, and both parents and teachers need to arouse curiosity and enable, as well as inspire, the desire to explore.

2.5 Motivation and emotional literacy

> *Motivation is the most important factor in determining whether you succeed in the long run. What I mean by motivation is not only the desire to achieve, but also the love of learning, the love of challenge and the ability to thrive on obstacles. These are the greatest gifts we can give our students.*
>
> (Dweck)

Children need to be motivated if they are to continue to self-educate at their own pace and find meaning through self-discovery. They now understands new concepts, with adults mediating less and less, but need to be stimulated to use their self-language-learning strategies to acquire, understand and eventually use a wider range of spoken English.

To motivate we need to arouse curiosity in children. Curiosity is aroused by seeing something new, or something different from what they expected. This arouses their interest to find more out about it. Children have an internal need for consistency, and they look for things to fit into their cognitive map of understanding. When something does not fit in, it causes tension or 'cognitive dissonance', which innately drives them to find out more so they can resolve the inconsistency and fit the new information into their thinking. During this process children are focusing, exploring and learning at a deep level, which researchers liken to a 'flow' experience (see Chapter 1, page 24). Highly curious people show openness to new ideas, as well as an innate drive to examine and learn, and therefore expand their own cognitive map.

I have no special talents. I am only passionately curious.

(Einstein)

Motivation and 'emotional literacy' are closely linked, and together help to create the 'feel-good factor' which is vital for self-learning. Goleman talks about emotional literacy as being the ability to experience and manage emotions positively, as well as recognise emotions in others and show empathy. If children of this age are not yet emotionally literate, it can be difficult to motivate them – and if they are not motivated, little or no self-acquisition of English can occur.

A child with little emotional literacy still finds the following activities difficult: working in pairs, group discussions, persuading, leading. Young children want and need to feel liked by other children in the class if they are to feel good.

Motivation can be thought of as 'intrinsic', where children motivate *themselves*, and 'extrinsic' where motivation comes from *outside* (with the teacher igniting it by setting the scene for an enabling activity).

> **It is accepted that the emotional mind can override the rational mind.**

(Anon)

To start to manage their emotions, children need to:

- feel physically secure and safe within the classroom
- feel the teacher understands and recognises their emotions
- know the classroom routine, so they can predict the next activity
- know some basic English to talk about their emotions
- know how to read emotions in others (children and adults).

Children need to be able to describe their emotions and thoughts in English if they are to develop a sense of well-being. If they have no simple vocabulary in English to express their emotions and thoughts, they may hide them or resort to talking about them in L1. If the teacher is not bilingual, he or she may not be able to understand unless another child is able to translate, or a parent tells the teacher. Words for feelings and thoughts can be picked up from teacher-talk – this can be in the form of teacher modelling, or from a planned game that introduces basic feelings in a context which children understand.

Children are constantly watching behaviour and learning how to show and handle their emotions through modelling and mirroring the teacher and other adults, as well as other children close to them. Consider this example:

Discussing feelings

- The teacher introduces words for describing emotions by cutting out cardboard face shapes and sticking them onto short sticks. Each cardboard face shape has a different facial expression drawn on it: a sad face, a happy face, a surprised face, an angry face, etc.
- The teacher shows the faces and asks the children to say how each face feels. The children learn to say *He's happy.* or *She's angry.* etc. They also learn to answer the question *Are you happy?* with *Yes, I'm happy.* or *No, I'm sad.*
- The teacher then plays a game with the children, calling out words to do with feelings and children have to choose the cardboard face that matches the word.

Good relationships with teachers and peers contribute to enjoyment. The teacher needs to include enabling activities in which children can work together. Children learn more from other children than from adults, since they are similar to themselves and easier to copy. However, they are constantly watching adults' behaviour and learning from it how to manage their emotions.

Emotions, and the way we show them to those around us, are culturally linked. Teachers should be aware, for example, that in some cultures a smile or laughter can cover up embarrassment or may be thought of as rude or inappropriate behaviour in class. In some L1 classrooms teachers may not expect children to show their emotions, so children have to be reassured that talking about feelings is *normal* and acceptable in the English classroom.

Within different cultures the use of silence, facial expressions, laughter and body language varies, and this should be carefully considered by teachers if they are to teach holistically – that is, to help the *whole* child mature.

When thinking about the emotional development of children, teachers need to include activities that help them begin to balance their emotions, such as using co-reading picture books that can be discussed together as a class. Free play, including book browsing, also helps children to self-manage their emotions. This is evident in the case of children (often boys) who like to learn to read through science books or books about their favourite imaginary superheroes.

Children need a rich language environment if they are to acquire language to their full potential and feel motivated. Motivation depends on the teacher's choice of structured enabling activities, appropriate to the interests and maturity of the children.

2.6 Monitoring and assessing

Regular assessing analyses the efficacy of activities and the teaching programme, as well as recording progress and highlighting the need for repetition and review. It is through regular assessment that teachers remain closely tuned-in to each child.

Children need to know that the teacher wants them to respond in English. To be responsive, they need to have no fear of making mistakes and need to be aware that mistakes can be used as an opportunity for learning. Children also need to know that the teacher understands risk-taking, and that he or she welcomes new suggestions and gives praise for effort. If children know that the teacher's response will always be positive, welcoming and encouraging, they will feel secure and begin to be responsive and show initiative. This is the best way for children to achieve their full potential in English.

As the child becomes more independent and confident, and more capable of taking responsibility in the classroom, the child–teacher relationship evolves into one of friendly, mutual respect. The child feels he or she can rely on the teacher to show personal understanding, listen to interests, welcome creative ideas and encourage efforts.

> *The only good kind of instruction is that which marches ahead of development and leads it.*
>
> (Vygotsky)

The teacher's role in helping learners reach their potential depends on the relationship with each child. For children to begin to develop their self-educating strategies, they needs to feel secure when taking risks and know that their opinions and efforts to learn are valued – by peers as well as the teacher.

> *The right kind of experience and support can help children to become confident, creative, motivated doers and thinkers so that the early years build a strong foundation for all they will encounter in the future.*
>
> (Stewart)

2.7 Teacher input

Interaction with adults through talk involves children in the adult's ways of thinking, and children's efforts to understand lead them to attempt to express similar meaning.

(Tough)

The child's innate aim is to speak as much English as possible and be able to read and write quickly. The child will, if motivated, be keen to use all the English they know and will find it frustrating when he or she is unable to convey thoughts, emotions and creative ideas.

The tuned-in teacher's role is to support children in achieving their goals by showing how and when to use English – bearing in mind this might be different from when and how their LI is used. For example, in some societies *please* and *thank you* are used differently from how they are used in English. Teachers cannot expect children to know that speaking in the lower-primary English classroom is welcomed, when in LI classrooms the teacher might be the only person who ever talks.

Although individual face-to-face contact is still important for conveying messages, lower-primary children can now follow the teacher when spoken to in pairs, groups or as a whole class. Spoken and written language needs to go beyond any actual text content – it needs to include the sharing of thoughts in order to help children begin to think of themselves as learners and critical thinkers. They need to be encouraged to initiate talking about their feelings, emotions and ideas. Children are innate communicators if they like the people they are talking to, and feel they are liked, too.

2.7.1 Teacher-talk

The use of voice is crucial to the success of a lesson. The teacher's commentary throughout the lesson (on what is taking place, what has been achieved and what is coming next) is a key part of input for revision, as well as for new spoken language. However, lower-primary children working together in pairs or small groups may also begin to talk amongst themselves in English. The teacher should encourage this, recasting what children have said and repeating it so all the class can hear. Teachers need to be ready to develop and expand any language produced by the children. For example: *Aisha says it's very cold today but Abdul says it isn't. What do you think?*

It is important not to over-question children as they soon begin to feel the teacher is giving them a test. Where possible, questions should be open-ended rather than having only a *Yes* or *No* answer. Open-ended questions lead to children giving a thoughtful and meaningful answer. Teachers should use *Wh-* question words whenever possible (*who, what, where, why, when, which,* etc.), for example:

What do you think about …?
Which is the best one?
What if he fell?
Where do you want to go? To the seaside, a big town, or somewhere else?
That's interesting. Why a big town?

The use of the teacher's voice is crucial:

- to convey a calm, warm, feel-good atmosphere
- to motivate and remotivate
- to make use of the Playful Approach
- to socialise behaviour
- to co-share in pair and group work
- to mediate and introduce new language activities
- to repeat target language
- to express emotion
- to encourage the use of English
- to reassure that ideas are valued.

2.7.2 Management language

The structures used in managing classroom activities are more complex with lower-primary children than with pre-school children. Management language has developed to include other situations, such as children playing games themselves in small groups, or taking part in responsible activities like tidying up.

Management language might sound like this: *Now it's tidy-up time. Hannah is collecting the pencils so please give your pencils to Hannah. Have you got all the pencils, Hannah?*

2.7.3 Mediating language

Mediating language can be used to introduce new formal literacy, or something brought to a 'My secret' session during 'Circle time' (see Chapter 6, page 97). Mediating language might be introduced as follows:

The teacher, during 'My secret', shows the children his or her favourite flower and introduces associated vocabulary, such as *flower, stalk, colour, roots,* etc.

The teacher links this vocabulary with *honey,* showing how a bee visits a flower.

She introduces *buzz* and *bumble bee,* so children can hear how the word *buzz* sounds like the noise the insect makes.

2.7.4 'Teacherese'

Teachers of young children often modify their speech (either by simplifying or including L1) when interacting with children who are still new to learning another language. This is known as 'teacherese'. Once children have a basic grounding in spoken English the amount of 'teacherese' needed diminishes, except when the teacher is introducing new language in an activity or in formal literacy. Although language content has increased by lower primary, the basic 'teacherese' strategies for dealing with code-switching and error correction remain the same.

A focused 'teacherese' session in a face-to-face dialogue can help comprehension greatly, particularly when a teacher finds a child has not understood and needs to revisit a topic.

2.7.5 Scaffolding

Scaffolding is a method of brainstorming, but in sustained, shared way. It helps children to focus and become conscious of their concentrated thought. Scaffolding can be used to revisit something that a child has not fully understood. Lower-primary children are more mature and they can scaffold with the teacher as a pair, in groups or as a class.

Co-thinking is exciting and motivating; it challenges a child, pair or group and takes them on to the next level. Often suggestions for follow-up ideas at home are included, for example the teacher might say *Look for a photo at home. Let's make a class book about …*

2.7.6 Repetition

Repetition gives a chance to try again. Children need to learn the saying *If at first you don't succeed try, try, and try again* (a saying originally popularised by Thomas H. Palmer in his *Teacher's Manual*). Children naturally *do* try and try again if they are interested and motivated. Watch them learning a skipping skill or repeating a physical game until they get it right! Teachers need to engage them repeatedly so they continue trying.

> *It takes time to build up a classroom routine and there are sessions when there seem to be steps backwards rather than forwards. This is normal in learning, and children may have absorbed more than outwardly visible in assessing.*
>
> (Stewart)

2.7.7 Tutor-talk

Hidden behind general teacher-talk is the planned, structured syllabus of the mechanics of language – these mechanics can sometimes be verbalised using 'tutor-talk'. The use of focused mini-tutorials can help children make progress at their own speed. Tutor-talk, although planned, can be introduced at any time within a lesson and can even be introduced further times within a lesson if appropriate. The teacher could say *Do you remember, I explained that this word means ...*

Quick tutor-talks can be used to revise a point introduced previously, to correct a recurring mistake, or to explain pattern variations. For example, the teacher might say *It's different this time. For this, we say ... Do you remember I said before that ...?*

It is through tutor-talk that the foundations of formal literacy are built. Quizzes and games may help to further pattern recognition, and a repertoire of these and other activities will help to consolidate the content of these mini-tutorials.

Piaget believed that learning depended on a child's readiness to learn. Vygotsky recognised a child's ability to learn with help.

2.7.8 Self-talk

The teacher's input can take the form of an external monologue of internal thinking. This form of 'self-talk' is quite usual among stressed adults who need to clarify their thoughts! Thinking through a problem, seeing cause and effect or weighing up risk is something children have to learn from adults. In self-talk teachers give more than a factual commentary – they reveal aloud how they actually think, feel and deal with a problem, in order to move towards making a decision. The teacher uses self-talk to show children how to think critically and sum up, before arriving at a choice or decision. If the decision is wrong, the teacher also uses self-talk to show how to go back and rethink, in order to arrive at a new decision or choice. For example, the teacher might say *Do I go here or do I go there? Oh dear! That's not right. I think I'll go back to the beginning. If I do this, what will happen?*

Through the teacher's regular repetition of these thinking-aloud language structures, children can absorb the language of thought and gradually begin to use it. Children, when encountering a problem, often give external monologues which reveal they have learned how to work through a decision-making process logically. A child might say *Let me think. Do I go here or do I go there? What if I do this? I'll try again. I have a good idea. What do I want — this or that? This is better.*

Once familiar with the basic language of thought, children begin to create their own personal thinking language, and may code-switch some words into L1. If this happens, the teacher needs to recast what the child has said in English.

> **Thought is internalised language.**
>
> (Vygotsky)

3

Listening to the maturing child

3.1 Self-educators

Helping children learn better is not the same as helping them become better learners.

(Claxton)

Young children are self-educators if they are provided with enabling experiences. From about 5 years old, many children show signs or wanting to do things for themselves. Many of them already want to become independent, saying things like *Let me try. I can do it.* They are active agents in their own learning and develop personal strategies to help them progress (including language-learning strategies, which – with adult help – they can reuse to acquire English).

By the age of 6, without being formally taught, children have managed to develop a range of self-learning strategies with which to learn many things. 'Learning to learn' involves knowing and being able to use these self-learning strategies effectively. Effective learning at this age forms the foundations for life-long learning.

Strategies are sequences of behaviour, which are developed to enable us to do things in more effective and efficient ways.

(Stewart)

By the age of 7, many of the self-learning strategies for acquiring language are in place, since children are by now fluent LI speakers. Children who already read and write in LI have also acquired some self-learning strategies for coded LI literacy.

As teachers, we need to foster young children's ability to self-learn, helping them to work out how to transfer their self-language-learning strategies to absorb English successfully. By now, children will already have unconsciously transferred their strategies to pick up spoken English, but they need help to do the same when learning how to read and spell and later create written English.

Learning to reuse and broaden strategies to acquire English cannot be taught by imposed instruction. Children have to explore and experiment for themselves, but they also need to be helped through focused tutor-talk explanations and modelling that they can imitate. Children need time to find out how to use their strategies to solve problems, self-manage and persevere to achieve progress.

To achieve there has to be volition, and for this children's inner drive needs to be ignited and continually stoked. To successfully orchestrate self-learning, teachers also have to monitor progress and assess by summarising, recalling and talking over how things were done and what was achieved. Listening to each other's reflections, ideas and questions is important, because – apart from being able to tell everyone about how they are thinking – children learn from watching and imitating their peers.

What children learn is important, but developing and becoming aware of their self-learning (and self-language-learning) strategies is even more crucial if children are to become life-long learners – including learners of English.

3.1.1 Reusing self-learning strategies

Learning English for a child is part of their holistic learning experience. Unless they are helped to build and reuse their self-learning strategies, children cannot progress effectively with their acquisition of English, or achieve further autonomy.

Focusing on how a young child learns is more important than the actual English language content that he or she acquires. Young children are innate, holistic language learners, if motivated, and unconsciously absorb language and use it. We don't force them to learn grammar rules, but through their own learning strategies young children work out grammar and – apart from pattern variations like saying *taked, doed, goed* instead of *took, did, went* – they often get it right!

The young child is becoming aware of *how* he or she learns, and is able to talk about this. The child is beginning to 'think about thinking' (metacognition), and needs to be listened to as he or she unconsciously reuses, adapts and broadens his or her self-learning strategies to acquire English. This growing awareness means that the child is developing strategies to self-assess and also assess the abilities of other children.

> *Whereas the child has to learn counting words for each language, she only has to learn the counting skill once. The skill is the same in each language and can therefore be transferred.*
>
> (Harding and Riley)

Teachers will need to use specific techniques — such as using 'teacherese', scaffolding and offering quick translations (see Chapter 2, pages 47–52) — to support children while they learn to transfer their self-learning strategies to the learning of English. As children's spoken English ability increases, these forms of support can be minimised until they are gradually faded out — except for use when introducing new material or supporting a slower learner.

Teacher's also need to be aware that any teaching outside their learners' 'zone of proximal development' ('ZPD' — see Chapter 2, page 41) may be ineffective. Teacher-imposed English language exercises which are not sensitive to a child's ZPD can probably be completed and learned by heart by most children, but many of those children will then find difficulty in transferring the content to other experiences and situations.

Teachers and parents should be careful not to over-support language acquisition as it can create dependency, whereby the child never takes the risk of making a mistake and always waits for support. As young children innately want to be independent, teachers need to encourage them to find out and try for themselves, using and developing their own personal strategies.

From about the age of 6 or 7, children start to become less egocentric and show more individuality and temperament. They like to take responsibility in coping with their freedom and are capable of thinking critically to make choices. Some parents who have a controlling bond over their children may not be aware of – or want to acknowledge – their child's growing maturity, and they might smoother their growth by not listening to them, by answering questions for them, and by constantly referring to their past interests and abilities instead of focusing on the present and the future.

3.1.2 Transferring strategies

> *Where one language is established before acquiring a second, strategies developed in learning the first language will transfer to the process of learning subsequent languages and be a positive aid to learning.*

(Tough)

Transferring strategies for reuse in English can be greatly helped by:

✓ Teacher-talk (explaining)
✓ Teacher modelling (showing how to use new language, or re-modelling known language to match new content)
✓ Teacher self-talk ('thinking aloud' to show how to work through ideas, solve problems, talk about strategies and manage emotions)
✓ Summing up activities (developing critical thinking)
✓ Asking open-ended questions (developing divergent thinking)
✓ Planning enabling, holistic activities and experiences
✓ Planning opportunities to work with other children in pairs or groups (imitating and learning)
✓ Listening to the child verbalise (valuing his or her way of thinking)
✓ Monitoring and observing activities (helping and encouraging effort)
✓ Assessing children's autonomy and ability to use their own strategies
✓ Listening to children's self-assessment and comments
✓ Listening to parents' assessment of their child

In addition, transferring formal literacy strategies for children who are already able to read in LI can be helped by:

* starting from the child's ZPD (zone of proximal development) in LI and English
* listening to the child verbalise how they think
* using tutor-talk (quick, focused explanations about language)
* using teacher-talk to help recognition of patterns and analogies.

When introducing gist understanding to English, teachers need to remember that children are still dependent on gist understanding strategies for acquiring new language in LI, using words, body language and their surrounding environment to piece together understanding. These strategies can be reused for English, but children need to build up confidence to use them successfully.

Teachers need to be aware that children do not need to understand every word in a sentence or utterance to make meaning. They are used to and satisfied with only understanding the gist of a text in LI, and transfer this acceptance to their understanding of English. Children also understand more than adults imagine and more than they can say. They also often use translation strategies to help each other in their understanding.

Consider these questions about children's self-learning strategies:

Q: Can self-learning strategies be taught by the teacher?
A: Not successfully, but they can be talked about and modelled. Children have to work out their own strategies by:

✓ taking part in holistic activities and games, enabling them to explore, experiment and imitate

✓ taking part in shared activities involving tutor-talk (explanation), modelling (show and talk) and self-talk (monologue commentary about problem solving and ways of thinking)

✓ interacting with other children and imitating.

Q: How can teachers find out what strategies children know and can reuse?

A: Teachers can know by:

✓ observing problem-solving techniques
✓ listening to children talking about doing and thinking (metacognition)
✓ listening to children's self-talk (monologue commentary)
✓ co-sharing, recalling and summarising
✓ talking about problem solving.

Teachers should look for these strategies in children:

- Self-management/self-regulation (including management of emotions, self-control, socialisation, control of effective learning, effort, concentration, critical thinking, achievement)
- Self-awareness (including thinking about: thinking, problem solving, attaining goals)
- Self-efficacy/ability as a learner (including self-correction and perseverance)
- Problem solving

Teachers can use the following types of open-ended questions to help children focus on thinking:

- *How did you do that?* (recall)
- *Can you do it another way?* (encouraging divergent thinking)
- *What was difficult?* (critical thinking)
- *Will you do it the same way next time?* (critical thinking)

Teachers should always value children's answers and points of view as this increases self-esteem and confidence. Children also need to be given time to reflect and reply.

3.2 Motivation

As young children mature they gradually develop and refine strategies to self-educate. When they reuse their strategies to cooperate with sensitive adults (who introduce stimulating, enabling, interactive activities) they can be even more successful.

Listening to children sensitively – giving them space to express their thoughts and way of thinking, and to respond to ideas – stimulates them. Children need to feel valued; it gives them energy to persevere and develop their autonomy and ownership. It also helps them understand their identity within the family, school and beyond.

> *How children learn is more important than what they learn.*
> *By showing children that we value their learning processes,*
> *we help them to reach confidently for opportunities to learn.*
>
> (Dweck)

Young children come to English lessons wanting and expecting to quickly read and write in English like they do in L1. For some, it is disappointing and frustrating that it takes time before they can express their thoughts and feelings in English. Emotional well-being underpins all development. Thus the teacher has to find a balance between motivation and the 'feel-good factor', remembering that cognitive intelligence is stable, but emotional intelligence has to be learned with help. Emotional control and management develops with a child's maturity. If an intelligent young child is emotionally not at ease, very little learning will take place.

Motivation is vital for success in language learning. Being a learner is not always easy; it requires effort at all ages. When children are motivated, they build up self-confidence and self-esteem, which stimulates and in turn remotivates. Motivation helps children resist other attractions and encourages them to focus.

Learning English is not only about acquiring knowledge. For children who have passed beyond the egocentric stage of development, feelings become more complex and involved, and ways of socialisation become wider and more profound. Other children's thoughts and words begin to influence a child's feelings. Without emotional and physical well-being, children find it difficult to develop the self-confidence to learn. Feeling positive underlies the attitudes and volition needed to persist with learning. Self-esteem, based on how others see us, is closely linked with motivation.

3.2.1 Mindsets

Psychologist Carol Dweck associates motivation with mindsets. She describes motivation as being either 'intrinsic' or 'extrinsic'. Intrinsic motivation comes from having an *internal* drive for autonomy which:

- stimulates interest
- produces a desire to achieve
- focuses concentration
- creates internal satisfaction/enjoyment on completion of a product or process.

Extrinsic motivation is influenced by *outside* achievements. It is motivated by gaining rewards and/or avoiding punishments or negative outcomes (for children, extrinsic factors are often something imposed by adults).

Dweck links a 'fixed mindset' to a product and a 'growth mindset' to a process. Her theory describes how fixed-mindset individuals dread failure as it is a negative statement on their basic abilities, whereas growth-mindset individuals do not fear failure because they realise their performance can always be improved. This theory is relevant to children and in classrooms we can see children developing both types of mindset. We can help children be more positive by the type of assessment we use with them, such as our choice of language when praising and encouraging.

> *Don't tell your kids that they are smart. More than three decades of research shows that a focus on effort – not on intelligence or ability – is key to success in school and in life.*
>
> (Dweck)

The 'feel-good factor' is important if children are to feel positive and able to use their strategies effectively. Without a balanced feeling of well-being children find it difficult to use their self-learning strategies effectively.

3.2.2 Changes which can affect learning

Many physical and emotional changes take place around the age of 6 and 7, and teachers need to be aware of these in order to empathise and keep children motivated.

Physical well-being

The way young children walk and hold themselves around the age of 6 or 7 demonstrates that they now feel more confident and grown up. About this age there are important physical changes in their bodies that can affect their feeling of well-being, sapping their energy and making focusing and learning language more difficult. Teachers need to be conscious of these changes and show empathy (for example, they should avoid asking a child to perform in front of others when the loss of a front tooth affects pronunciation). Children can be critical of each other, especially when showing empathy to others has not yet been discussed in class.

Differences between the physical needs and interests of boys and girls are increasing at this lower-primary age and becoming more obvious. All children need to move around regularly to maintain concentration, but teachers often find that boys in particular need a lot of opportunities to release energy! This needs to be kept in mind when planning lessons. Many boys also have passionate interests in superheroes, comic-book characters, adventures stories, cars, science, space and sporting celebrities. To keep boys motivated teachers need to feed these interests.

Some boys complain that they don't feel good in the English classroom and don't like learning English. Some complain that the atmosphere is too feminine and many of the activities are too 'girlie'. They are not comfortable when there are too few male role models to copy, or too few opportunities to hear a male voice speaking English – other than the boys in the class.

Physical differences between boys and girls also influence their language learning strategies. Some of the ongoing physical changes that can affect learning are:

- body size (sudden changes of height and muscle development)
- muscular control of new growth areas, especially hand control
- hand–eye coordination for reading and handwriting
- growth of mouth cavity (the sound-box area)
- loss of first teeth and new growth of adult teeth and molars, affecting pronunciation
- hearing difficulties caused by growth of adult teeth.

Emotional well-being

Children's strategies for self-management are developing and teachers will find that children's ability to balance these strategies can vary from day to day, depending on their emotional well-being.

Daniel Goleman outlines the main developing strategies involved in emotional Intelligence:

- Self-monitoring and self-reflecting
- Self-managing emotions (self-focusing, self-motivating, management of: stress, excitement, sadness, happiness)
- Empathy (understanding and caring for others)
- Social inter-relations with others (inspiring, collaborating, sharing)

3.3 Evaluating success

3.3.1 Praising children

> *Adult comments should focus on the goal of learning rather than on the level of outcome of their performance. Growth mindset is important.*

> (Dweck)

Talking about the learning process is usually more important than the final product or outcome. However, teachers should remember that learning is a triangle which includes parents and extended family, and the product is often regarded as important proof of a child's achievement. Parents' positive reaction to a product can stimulate; children look for parents' approval and praise as it helps them confirm that what they are doing is right.

In talking about *success* teachers need to focus on *effort*, and how to achieve goals. Helping children verbalise their own effort and the learning process can be encouraged by using a type of scaffolding, where the teacher leads the interaction, introducing new language and thinking. The teacher might say, for example:

> *Then what did you do? Oh, you joined it up.*
> *Did you use a ruler and pencil? Why was it difficult?*
> *Because of the pencil?*

It is better not to over-praise achievement, especially for an activity which may have been easy for the child. Instead, encourage the child to try something new and praise effort where there has been a particular challenge involved. The teacher might say A *really good try, Emiko. Now try again. You can make it even better!*

When praising children, teachers need to show that they value individual learning processes. They need create opportunities for children to take responsibility, so that children can discover how challenge – and even difficulty – can be very motivating.

3.3.2 Assessment by adults

Without listening, observing and assessing, teachers cannot extend children's learning strategies or meet their need for repetition. Teacher's need to remember that:

- Children sometimes behave in a different way at school than they do at home. They can also behave differently in English classes than they do in L1 classes – particularly if the classes have different teachers.

- Parents may be surprised by their child's developing abilities in English, especially if they are not 'shown off' at home.
- Parents may label children saying (in front of the child) things like *He's shy. He's no good at games.* These labels can be incorrect as some children merely perform to conform to their parents' descriptions (see Chapter 2, page 42).

> *Observational assessment enables teachers to intervene, support and extend a very young child's learning ability as it is happening. It will inform planning for the next steps in learning for each child, deepening and extending the child's learning.*
>
> (United Kingdom Department for Education and Schools)

Maturity at this young age partly depends on the local culture and how society regards 'childhood'. This influences the type of enabling activities children will experience and the aspirations of the parents. This said, technology is bringing the world into homes and changing children's experiences. Even if the screen experience is not interactive, many young children have developed self-learning strategies to pick up some English, for example from dialogues. However, they are not always sure of the meaning or when and how to use it in real life.

Teachers might think of themselves as being employed to follow a set syllabus, but they also need to be tuned in to children's use of self-learning strategies, as well as their interests and levels of development. Without this tuning-in, a teacher cannot be a successful co-dialoguer – and children need interaction to pick up ideas and language. At the lower-primary age it is easy to recognise a child's physical milestones, but for successful learning to take place teachers need to be constantly assessing a child's emotional and social maturity, as well as his or her innate desire for knowledge and autonomy (which is intrinsically linked to the use of self-learning strategies).

Teachers need evidence from regular ongoing assessments to show that children are acquiring knowledge (content) *and* the language to talk about what and how they learn. By this age children are ready to discuss and summarise what they are doing and how they have performed, comparing their achievements with previous attempts and the work of others.

> *It is difficult to sustain interest in an activity unless one achieves some degree of competence.*
>
> (Bruner)

Children and their parents need to be made aware that they are making progress as this stimulates and motivates them. With developing maturity children begin to regularly self-assess, as well as assessing the progress of others in the class (see 3.3.3 below). Teachers may hear children say *He's the best at translating. She not very good at drawing.* In some cases their self-assessment might be incorrect and demotivating, especially when they perceive their peers' work to be of a higher standard. Teachers must work closely with children to check these self-assessments and to harness any disappointment, using it in a positive way to create self-motivation to do better next time.

Above all, teachers need to respect children's desire to develop autonomy. The skilled teacher's task is to balance the provision of stimuli with the support of autonomy.

Valid assessment takes time and should include these elements:

- Knowing a child well and regularly judging their degree of autonomy
- Providing high-quality, regular one-to-one interaction
- Recording a child's involvement, effort, persistence, self-satisfaction, positive mindset and 'feel-good factor'
- Knowing a child's listening, understanding and speaking ability, as well as their level of confidence
- Being aware of a child's ability to understand 'gist'
- Engaging parents' support (especially the child's mother, who is usually – but not always – the main L1 teacher)

Although any assessment cannot be completely accurate as every child knows more than they can express verbally, assessments are invaluable for planning repetition and for structuring the introduction of new material.

> *As adults our passive vocabulary is usually a third larger that our active vocabulary. We understand far more than we routinely use.*
>
> (Crystal)

Quick assessments after each lesson – or even notes made during a lesson – help to identify the necessary next steps for a child's holistic learning and English progress. These kinds of ongoing quick assessments also help teachers to identify any guidance needed for effective planning and follow-up in the next few lessons.

3.3.3 Self-assessment

Young children have already developed an accurate ability to self-assess, which is an important step in learning how to learn (metacognition). Children assess whether they are making progress and also self-assess their position in the class. They know who is good at what and need time to discuss their assessments with other children. Teachers can learn from their discussions, which may reveal different points of view from their own! Most children know how to work hard to meet their own goals, which in turn reinforces their self-motivation.

To self-evaluate and confirm self-confidence, young children need:

- space and time for self-correction and self-reflection (process)
- opportunities to 'show off' progress to other adults and children (product – including spoken language, reading, rhymes, songs, spelling quiz results or project work).

3.4 Autonomy

Froebel and Montessori both discuss how young children – as they develop beyond the egocentric stage around 5 years old – show an innate desire to be independent. They are developing their own self-learning strategies and continually refining their language-learning strategies. They begin to think independently; they know when help is needed and they ask for it. They are prepared to be tutored (tutor-talk) but, once something is shown and understood, they want to try it for themselves. Later, as they gain more confidence, they even watch other children model something and, unaided, they imitate it themselves.

For learning to be effective, teachers need to constantly monitor the changing levels of children's self-learning strategies and also respect children as they gradually become autonomous learners. Young children's innate drive to develop autonomy (independence) requires understanding, time, patience and supportive encouragement on the part of teachers and parents. Children are so thrilled when they can say *Look ... I did it all by myself!*

A child's progress towards learner autonomy depends on:

- innate self-motivation
- the 'feel-good factor' (physical and emotional well-being, within a safe environment)
- the amount and quality of exposure to spoken and written language
- the quality of language interaction with adults and older children
- effective enabling activities in which to reuse and broaden their strategies.

> *The bilingual child learns two languages in the same way and in the same order as the monolingual child learns one, with the obvious difference that the bilingual child has to learn to distinguish between the two.*
>
> (Harding and Riley)

4

Cooperating with parents

4.1 Tuning in

The importance of the parents' role in shepherding a child's acquisition of English, especially in the beginning stages of a more formal approach, is often overlooked by teachers. Parents are usually children's first language teachers and obviously have a special bond with them, and children in turn want to please their parents and need their love. Parents know their children best and intuitively decode their feelings and needs, as well as their 'winding-up' tricks.

> *It is obvious that the great majority of parents are their children's first carers, but we now find a broad agreement that parents are also their children's first and most enduring educators.*
>
> (Whitehead)

Many parents need help to tune in to their child's English learning as they are not always aware of how well children are capable of absorbing English, or of new educational research relevant to learning English as L2. Teachers could consider preparing a presentation or written document explaining to parents:

- how their children will be taught
- how their children will be prepared for tests, if they have to take them
- how they can best support their children.

Teachers often forget that most parents lack confidence, as they feel they are treading a new path that they may not understand. Many parents need encouragement and some may not even realise that any positive interest they show can help to motivate their child.

Cooperation between teacher and parents is vital since any criticism of the teacher or teaching methods can quickly spread. Children talk amongst themselves, saying things like *My mother says that the English teacher is ...* , which is then repeated to other parents! Young children are still very influenced by what their parents say. Even if criticism is not verbalised, children can still feel it from their parents' body language and attitudes.

The balance of the triangle of child, parent and teacher still remains important if the English learning environment is to be right for the child. By now English learning has spread beyond the teacher and classroom to other children and teachers in the school. It may also have spread to the extended family and influenced wider aspects, like the family occasionally eating British food!

Regular assessment with photos, texts or even recordings can help children to feel that they have a role to play in the triangle. Homework and preparation for regular spelling quizzes also help parents feel they are making a purposeful and satisfying contribution.

4.2 Parents' involvement

Teachers' interaction with adults through talk involves children in the adult's ways of thinking and children's efforts to understand lead them to attempt to express similar meaning.

(Tough)

4.2.1 Parent power

Parents can have a lot of influence (sometimes called 'parent power'). Most parents are very interested in their child, and a positive attitude from parents is important for the child's success. Parents want to help and can do so even if they have only basic English themselves – but they often lack confidence. They may say things like *My pronunciation is no good. I can't get my r's and l's right.*

Teachers can guide parents, harnessing their 'power' to undertake supportive activities in the home. This helps parents to tune in to their children. There can be joy in learning together as a family and surprises too, when parents hear their 7-year-old son or daughter correct their pronunciation! Parents often relay their experience to the teacher, who then needs to remind parents that young children already have skills to critically compare the difference in English sounds … a remarkable linguistic achievement at the age of 7!

To attain a positive balance, the teacher needs to keep parents regularly informed of how and what he or she is teaching. The teacher also needs to be ready for regular feedback – good and bad – and any criticism needs to be dealt with immediately. Parents who are tuned in to their child have intimate current knowledge of him or her, not least because they see homework taking place and often participate in it. However, teachers need to decode whether a parent is interpreting their child through their own ideas, or reporting the child's reactions accurately.

> *Parents are more knowledgeable about their own children than anyone else can ever be; they have a deeper emotional commitment to them and wider background of experience shared with them than can ever be achieved in institutions, which have the children for a comparatively few hours.*
>
> (Whitehead)

4.2.2 The Playful Approach at home

The English teacher skilfully uses the Playful Approach to keep levels of motivation high (see Chapter 1, page 19), as he or she builds on children's strategies and gradually introduces formal literacy. Parents probably recognise that they also used a similar approach when their children were very young; they can capitalise on this by now using the Playful Approach to motivate their lower-primary children to do their homework and learn their spellings. Some homework and special projects can be started off in class and finished at home, with parents supporting and encouraging their child to stay motivated, thus enhancing enjoyment.

Play is recognised as the highest form of learning. It helps children to apply what they have learned in an integrated way. However, it is not the only effective and appropriate way that a child learns. The freedom to play is often confused with the playful methods that parents use when motivating their child to explore and acquire a more formal skill or persevere to complete a task.

> *There is confusion about what learning through play actually means and what the implications of this are for the role of adults.*

(Tickell)

The confusion over play is one of the many things that need explaining to parents if they are to understand how their child acquires formal literacy skills. Parents need to understand that their child needs space and time in order to find out that effort and perseverance get results. Even playing the same game over and over again with a parent until they win contributes to children's self-discovery and self-management!

> *Genius is one per cent inspiration, ninety-nine per cent perspiration.*

(Edison)

4.2.3 Sharing with parents

That fact that parents keenly follow their child's progress is clearly good for the child. It is up to the teacher to harness this interest by explaining to parents *how* children are acquiring English in the classroom. Teachers also need to give parents confidence through useful suggestions for follow-up at home.

Parents need to be able to experience their child's progress. To do this, teachers need to include 'show off' pieces, like rhymes, songs or jokes that can be enjoyed by the entire family. These quick, oral experiences convince parents of some progress.

Parents are also often involved in more formal spelling quizzes that show weekly progress. Where possible, picture books can be taken home for shared reading, or suggestions can be made for suitable English-speaking YouTube video clips to be watched and enjoyed together at home.

Many parents also enjoy working with their child on English projects. For example, research on a particular topic might start at home supported and supervised by parents, then be developed, finished and displayed at school. Finally, the end result can be taken home for children to show their extended family. These kinds of special projects help parents to share and participate in their child's English-learning experience.

4.3 Teaching for a test

Passing an English test is an accepted passport to the next stage in education in some countries, and especially in Asia. Although the teacher may not fully agree with testing at this age, he or she has to compromise and accept the local context, preparing children with the test strategies needed for success. By doing this the teacher is building on children's existing strategies to absorb language, giving children a new set of strategies and the confidence to perform well in a different and stressful situation.

Parents need to be aware of the differences between an English-experience classroom and the type of teacher-led instruction / rote-memorising that is geared towards testing. Focusing only on teaching and revising for tests (which measure children's present level but not their potential) can be boring and demotivating for the child unless a playful approach is judiciously inserted. The attitudes formed through boredom and parents pushing for top marks may not show at this early stage, but may appear later in adolescence, when children have the power to reject what they do not like or wish to do.

If children have followed a hidden syllabus with rich input via teacher-talk and tutor-talk – and also been given opportunities to interact using English – they can usually understand and speak more English than is required for a test. Despite this, short, focused pre-test preparation is essential as it:

- gives confidence to the child and to their parents (avoids damaging, infectious stress)
- gives information on how to manage the test (test skills are different from routine absorbing and using of English)

- revises the expected set pieces of English (words, phrases and simple sentences)
- can provide role-play experience with a native-speaker 'examiner' (an invited guest or parent).

If prepared in this way, young children generally achieve the required result, taking the challenge in their stride and without feeling bored. Parents are sometimes surprised by the results of the test, saying things like *The examiner was amazed that my son replied so confidently when talking about his feelings. She said he has a big vocabulary for his age. My child's teacher speaks English all the time, so that's why he feels so confident.*

4.4 Bringing English into the home

Parents have to develop an enabling attitude to using English by creating a 'talking English relationship'. In this relationship, the child wants to and enjoys talking in English to family members, often at a regularly scheduled time. The 'feel-good factor' is very important for all learning, and especially for learning a language since it involves dialoguing with someone older who is sensitive to you and what you say.

Learning and sharing English experiences in a family can be bonding. English phrases sometimes become private 'in-family' language over several generations, recalling experiences with deeper meaning.

Talking to their child face-to-face *about* English or *in* English can encourage and motivate both the parent and the child. This requires patience. Too often adults are rushed and do not give children time to reply, smothering a child's English by finishing off sentences, talking for them and giving answers. This can demotivate. For example, when playing a game a parent might say *You've got a blue card. Put it there ...* rather than *What have you got? Shall we put it here or there?*

Homework can be blended into home English time or may be separate, depending on the formality of the homework task. However, all tasks will be easier if parents use a playful approach, remembering not to correct mistakes since any criticism may temporarily stunt an enabling atmosphere (see Chapter 1, page 23). Homework can involve the use of recordings on phones or tablets to help parents with pronunciation where needed.

How parents can bring English into the home

✓ Make an 'English Corner' (see Chapter 11, page 228). By now children can enjoy simple written text so continually introduce new items.

✓ Make sure there is paper, pencils and coloured pens always available in a known place for writing, drawing or copying.

✓ Cut out photos from newspapers or download them from the Internet. Add English headings to them.

✓ Have a special time (separate from homework time) when you sing songs or say rhymes children already know in English.

✓ Download songs in English so children can play them on a tablet or smartphone.

✓ Collect words written in English within the environment.

✓ Cook or buy some English food. Have an 'English-speaking meal' with dishes from the English-speaking world.

✓ Reuse and adopt English phrases from stories, songs or rhymes, making them into in-family language, such as *No, not now. In a few minutes. No problem. You can do it. Go ahead.*

✓ Watch selected YouTube videos in English together, making a commentary.

✓ Play board games together. Make up your own games inserting your in-family words, for example names of seaside creatures.

✓ Play games to decide who does something.

✓ Read stories, picture books, and information books together.

✓ Create a non-stressed haven at home where children can freely play, browse, reflect and consolidate.

4.5 Assessments for Parents

Parents need to see and hear progress as well as receive formal teacher assessments. Formal assessments should, however, be regular – if possible, once a week or once every two weeks. They can be:

- visual (photos or samples of written work or handwork)
- recorded (on tablets or smartphones)
- textual plus visual (such as email newsletters).

Special 'wow' moments when a child does something outstanding or, through effort, makes a significant leap forward need to be recorded in a special way within the classroom and reported to the parents on that same day.

End-of-term or end-of-year performances are expected by many schools as well as parents. These can be a form of assessment, although for the teacher the preparation activities are often more important than the final productions. Associated activities include making tickets, programmes and posters, and giving children opportunities to play different roles. A production or show can be an opportunity for children to learn a whole script by heart and even prompt each other effectively where necessary. For children a performance is also an opportunity to have their parent's total attention and interest, and this is stimulating and motivating for future learning.

Above all, care should be taken that assessing does not become too time-consuming and therefore take away from interactive sharing activities with the teacher and/or other children.

> *The function of words include enjoyment as well as communication.*
>
> (Crystal)

5

Planning, managing and assessing

5.1 Planning lessons

Young children thrive on structure, consistency and routine. It makes them feel good. They feel in control of the situation as they can predict the pattern of the lesson, rather than insecurely waiting for things to happen.

The world seen through children's eyes is not divided into compartments or shown on a timetable as 'subjects'. English for a young child is another tool for communicating about themselves and their world. To teach young children English successfully, we need to understand child development. Without this background knowledge it is difficult to accurately respond to individual children's changing holistic needs or their desire to be helped to do things on their own.

Many of today's children are stressed and some bring their stress to school with them. They need teachers to listen to them and an adult showing caring interest seems to help them manage their emotions. In some cases, a few words of welcome, face-to-face in English, are sufficient to relax a child enough to enjoy a lesson. Learning English can be an additional frustration for some young children as it takes time and effort before children can use English to talk about themselves and their interests. 'My secret' sessions can help, as individual presentations can introduce words and expressions to talk about emotions and social behaviour (see Chapter 6, page 97). Teacher-talk can also introduce expressions that can help children to communicate feelings and worries.

The English teacher is often friendlier and more relaxed than some other subject teachers at school. Despite this, frustration can build if the English teacher does not speak L1 and the children have not yet acquired enough English of their own. This frustration is present in some young children's English classrooms and often passes unrecognised by teachers; it can be a reason why some children cannot manage to focus.

5.1.1 Having a framework

Children appear to learn more easily when they know what to expect in a lesson and what the teacher expects of them. Apart from making

Figure 1 A class framework

Phase	Aim	Activities	Place
Introduction	Cultivate 'feel-good factor'	Welcome individuals	Classroom door
Phase One Class activities	Warm up Introduce personal things (teacher and child)	Revision of oral play including rhymes My secret Introduce new language	On mat, sofa or sitting round teacher's chair
Phase Two Individual or small group activities	Completing new activities / consolidating at own level	Practical activity Spelling quiz Tutor-talk	Sitting at own place or moving around the classroom
Phase Three Class or small group games, projects, drama or other activities	Further consolidating experiences	Projects, language games, Free choice	In an open space or sitting in groups
Ending	Cultivate 'feel-good factor'	Class tidies up then sits on the mat Discussion about and show of day's work Summarise, Review homework Repeat rhymes, sing 'goodbye' song Teacher says goodbye and adds a personal comment to each child	Mat, sofa or at own place Classroom door

them feel more secure, it enables them to predict the situations and language likely to be used. For this reason, teachers find it helpful to be consistent and use the same framework and management language for each session or lesson, adjusting the content to match children's reactions, progress and learning needs.

Why use a class framework?

- It forms the basis of a routine that is followed in each lesson. Activities are then slotted into the framework.
- As a known routine, it creates a 'feel-good factor', giving children confidence to move on to the next stage of a lesson. They may even make preparations for the next stage themselves before the teacher has given instructions.
- The feeling of familiarity enables children to focus on an activity free from the stress of not knowing what to do next. The calm buzz of a class during a familiar routine is quite noticeable when compared with a haphazardly planned lesson with little regular routine.
- The known routine enables young children to gradually take over responsibilities to manage class activities, freeing the teacher to focus on children who need extra face-to-face scaffolding.

5.1.2 Planning a 'hidden syllabus'

A well-planned lesson involves planning the English language the teacher wants to include. Without links to this 'hidden syllabus', enabling experiences can remain at the same level with few new cognitive or linguistic acquisition opportunities.

To plan effectively it is easiest to break the term plan into smaller units. As well as individual lesson plans, teachers need weekly and monthly plans, which then fit into the larger term and/or year plan.

While planning the teacher also needs to include homework activities. Homework can provide children with an opportunity to finish off something started in class which they know and understand. Homework gives children an opportunity to be independent and do something by themselves, in their own way and time. It might even involve them in a 'flow' experience (see Chapter 1, page 24).

Using a hidden syllabus does not mean that a teacher is not listening to children's language or ideas and following them. If teachers are following a textbook, selected activities can complement the textbook language and provide children with more personal language to talk about themselves. Classroom activities can act as a bridge between the textbook and the children, helping them increase their spoken ability and also their efficacy in using their self-learning strategies. Children won't be inspired to think about thinking and develop creativity just by reading a large number of texbooks. This will come instead from the interactive, playful atmosphere of the classroom, from the focused use of language, and from the enabling, creative activities orchestrated by the teacher.

5.2 Managing the autonomous learner

By now the young child has matured holistically and understands much more English than he or she can speak. Parents and teachers often underestimate how much young children understand by gist, and they under-play opportunities for children to use their strategies to decode spoken English. Teachers or parents might say *That's too difficult for him.* or *She doesn't understand.* Homework should not be a test that has to be finished correctly. It does not matter if the child cannot do it since any errors simply show a teacher where to give more support. The important thing is that the child made an effort and was not demotivated.

Figure 2 A suggested Hidden Syllabus

Item	Examples	Accompanying questions
Numbers		*How many? How much?*
Alphabet		
Colours	*brown, blue, green, orange, etc.*	*What colour is this/that?*
Nouns	• classifications (some things are uncountable like water • with indefinite articles (*a* or *an*) • with definite article (*the*) • plural nouns	*What's this?* *Where's the …?* *How many are there?*
Conjunctions	*and, or*	*Is this a … or a ….?*
Verbs	*to be (I am …), to have got (I've got …)* simple present	affirmative and negative question forms *Are you?* *Aren't you?*
Prepositions of place	*in, on, under, neart*	*Where is it?* *Where are they?*
Imperative for instructions	*Stop, Go, up, turn right/left* (affirmative) *Don't stop. Don't turn right* (negatives)	
Adjectives	big, little, sad, happy, etc	
Pronouns Subject pronouns Possessive pro-nouns	*I, you, he, she, we, you, they* *my, yours, his, hers, its, ours, theirs*	*Who* *Whose?*
Verbs	*want + noun want an apple, don't want an apple* *want + infinitive want to go, don't want to go*	*Does he want a bat?* *Does he want to go?*
Verbs	*can + infinitive can run, can jump, can't run*	*Can he dance?*

Verbs	*like + noun like bananas, like ice-cream, don't
	  like bananas*
	*like + verb like playing the piano, don't like
	  playing the piano*
		Do you like bananas?
		
		Does she like playing the piano?

Item	Examples	Accompanying questions
Time	days of the week parts of the day (*morning, afternoon, evening, night*) meal time hours and minutes months and years seasons	*When?* *What time is it?*
Nouns for the family	*mother, father, sister, brother, etc*	*Who is …?*
Nouns for parts of body	*leg, arm, head, etc*	
Nouns for clothes	*T-shirt, dress*	*Whose is ….?*
Nouns for home	rooms (*kitchen*, etc.), furniture (*sofa, bed*, etc.)	
Prepositions for transport	*by bus, on foot*	*How did you go?*
Classifiers	*a piece of, a bottle of, a glass of, a box of, etc*	
Veb forms Present continuous Simple past Future	**affirmative** **negative** *I am eating* *I am going* *I went* *He didn't come* *He will buy* *I won't go* *I am going to sneeze* *He isn't going to get a book*	*Are you listening?* *Did you win?* *Will you ask?* *Are you going to come with me?*
Professions	*a doctor*	*What is he/she* *What are they?*
Places	*station, supermarket, hospital*	*Where is ….?* *Where does he work?*
Adverbs	*slowly, quickly, now, soon, sometimes, here, there*	*How?* *When?* *Where?*
Adjectives Comparative Superlative	*smaller* *smallest*	*Which is smaller?* *Which is the smallest?*
Irregular adjectives	*good, better, best*	*Is this better?*

Young children are proud of their self-management strategies – organising themselves, their school bags, their lunch boxes. If children feel positive about themselves and their lives, they begin to show signs of:

* taking control of their own learning (autonomous learning) and beginning to think about thinking (metacognition).
* socialising and interacting, not only in pairs but in small groups (learning from other children can be more effective than learning from the teacher).
* decoding and encoding text, enjoying formal activities like a spelling quiz.
* understanding that initiative and divergent thinking is appreciated by the teacher.
* carrying on 'private talk' (thinking aloud – see Chapter 1, page 28), knowing it is valued and accepted.
* allowing time for individual thinking, browsing and reflection, which can be stimulated to continue at home or expanded by being shared with others.
* allowing time for shared thinking, in a pair or in a group, to solve a problem.

Young children can self-assess and know if they are making progress. They cannot pick up language if they cannot listen to it and too often there are long silences in an English-learning classroom, of the type that rarely occur when a mother is teaching her child to speak L1. Children need a rich language environment and are capable of absorbing more than adults imagine. However, they can also switch off if there is an uninteresting overload.

5.2.1 Pair or group work

Although face-to-face exchanges with the teacher are still very important, the more mature child can now learn from interaction with the teacher when working as a pair or in a small group.

Working in pairs or groups within a class may be a new way of learning for some children and even within some schools. In some societies, children are taught from pre-school to respond as a whole class rather than individuals. It is important to understand the norms and expectations of the local education system in order to know how best to introduce and structure a more interactive style. These are some points to consider as a teacher:

- The school style of teaching may be very different to what is happening in the English classroom; it may be predominantly teacher-led, to the whole class, with little appreciation of self-initiative.
- Cultural customs can create competition between families and their children, which can make socialising and sharing more difficult.
- Cultural expectations of what progress in English looks like can vary.
- Cultural ways of behaving and approaches to discipline may be different.

Teachers should build up towards working in pairs or small groups, as it is an important step in developing children's growing desire to become more independent learners. It also gives teachers an opportunity to co-dialogue with individual children, whilst other children are working together. Where children are not used to working this way, teachers need to structure the introduction to an activity by partnering with a child, modelling how to share the activity. The organisation of pairs should initially be done by the teacher as it is important that one child in each pair has more English so they can lead and even teach the other.

Teacher:	*You do it first.*
Child:	*Where shall I cut?*
Teacher:	*Cut there* [pointing], *on the line.*
Child:	*There, now what shall I do?*
Teacher:	*Give it to me, I'll show you. Here …*

After modelling pair work, and once children begin to work confidently in pairs, the teacher can then model group work. It is often a good idea to model the first group with more mature children who are ready to take responsibility. These children can then act as leaders of other groups, cascading knowledge and orchestrating language.

A well-run classroom, where all children are confidently busy and are participating at their maximum learning level, takes time to build up.

Without teachers moving round commenting and remotivating, these forms of class management may not be successful. Teachers have to be prepared for off days when things do not go so well. On these occasions it is good to have a brainstorming session in the summing-up time at the end of the lesson, suggesting together how to manage better next time. It is important to listen to children, as they have their own ideas and are beginning to think critically. However, they may need help in formulating their ideas in English. The teacher can do this by reflecting back what they are trying to say and then repeating it to the whole class.

> Girl: *Mae says Hong shouts.*
> Hong: *I don't shout.*
> Mae: *Yes, you do.*
> Teacher: *Let's all try to talk quietly next lesson, OK?*
> Class: *OK.*

5.2.2 Lesson essentials

The key to being able to teach effectively is good preparation of content, based on assessment. This enables a teacher to confidently concentrate on orchestrating language opportunities and managing his or her classroom.

The basic framework of the lesson remains largely the same to give children a sense of security (see 5.1.1), but the length of the phases can be adapted to fit content and the children's level of focus each day. There should be fixed times every week for the spelling quiz and the 'My secret' session, as children need time to prepare (part of the *process*) for these tasks (the *product*). Impromptu activities, like a quick game or rhyme, can be inserted without pre-planning to regain focus as it begins to wander.

Beginning and ending lessons

The social function of greeting people and saying goodbye, although limited linguistically, allows the teacher to have personal contact with each individual child at the beginning and end of each lesson. An experienced teacher uses this moment to get a sense of a child's mood at the beginning of the lesson and to add a few words of encouragement if necessary. At the end of a lesson, the teacher can send the child home with a comment on his or her participation as well as some encouraging suggestions about how to do the homework. Young children look forward to these special times with their friendly teacher. The teacher's few words are very important to them; they also play an important part in keeping children motivated.

Summing up at the end of a lesson

Recapping what has been done in the lesson and suggesting what can be done as follow-up in the next session are important methods of consolidating. Summing up also makes children feel secure. They know what to expect – but not completely, as a good teacher includes one or two exciting surprises to be discovered next time!

5.2.3 Class rules

> *Feeling part of a community and learning its rules and expectations helps children learn how they can contribute to what goes on and rise to the challenge of what it offers.*
>
> (Engel)

For a class to work well, children need to understand what type of behaviour the teacher expects of them. At the beginning of the school year, and maybe at the beginning of each term, it is important to discuss class rules, with children modelling where necessary.

We cannot expect children to take responsibility, organise and share in a classroom if they have no model in their mind. Imitating a model is one of the main ways young children know how to learn. They might say *Show me how. How do I do it?* Showing with accompanying language is vital for understanding. It can sometimes be difficult for adults to get down to the young child's level and understand the type of help they need. One way they can do this is to imagine being in a foreign language class, where the cultural background is completely different.

Many schools write out class rules on a sheet of paper or card and display them for all to read. Teachers also give copies of the rules to parents as they often like to know about the type of discipline expected in the English classroom. Sometimes these socialising English rules are even adopted as home rules. In one household *Wait your turn please!* became part of family table talk!

Class Rules

1. I will be friends with everyone and think about how they feel.
2. I will not touch other children's work without saying *Please*.
3. I will put up my hand when I want to say something or ask a question.
4. I will not talk when someone else is talking. I will wait for my turn.
5. I will share other children's happiness when we play games.
6. I will always tidy up.
7. I will do my homework. I will get ready for the spelling quiz.
8. I will tell the teacher when I have a problem.

Modelling good behaviour and *showing* how is important, as children may have no image (or a different cultural image) on which to base their personal behaviour. For example, helping some children cope with losing in a game (Rule 5) can take time. They have to realise that fair play is honourable and cheating is not acceptable! To understand losing, children need help to separate their mistakes from who they are. Mistakes are something made in the game and we all can learn from our mistakes.

> *I try to teach my students that losing is something you do, not something you are.*

(Spiegel in Tough)

Simple rules for behaviour and socialising help children to bond as a class. It gives them tools and language to be effective when cooperating with others and socialising in a wider community. It also helps them to think as a group and not always as an individual, developing their self-control strategies. Feeling part of a group gives them a sense of security that contributes to their 'feel-good factor'. Use sentences like *Anna, can you help Joe, please? What is wrong with Pat? Our class always says 'thank you'. Put your hand up. Did you say 'please' to her?*

5.2.4 Taking responsibility

Children want to take more responsibility in the classroom and if they are given instructions and shown what is expected, the enjoy fulfilling responsible tasks. They like to know what is required of them the lesson before so they have time to think beforehand about how they will manage. In many cases, the process of anticipating how to cope is almost as important as the actual carrying out of the duty. A teacher could say *Next lesson Maria is charge of the pencils and Edwardo is in charge of tidying the book corner.*

5.2.5 Collecting materials

It is too big a task to collect materials just before a lesson. Teachers need to become constant collectors, keeping an eye open at all times for suitable creative materials. The Internet has changed the teaching of young children as teachers now have the chance to download a vast range of material, including fonts, texts and images. Apart from this, there is free information to support teachers and allow them to self-educate. Most teachers have a bank of materials that they can draw on at any time to support an activity or create a project.

Clips from YouTube can also be used as support in a lesson, but these need to be researched and set up beforehand so as not to waste valuable learning time.

5.3 Self-assessment

It is good for teachers to step back and assess themselves from time to time. They should also attempt to assess their children's 'feel-good factor' – not just their progress. Visual assessments, such as photos, can sometimes be quite revealing. Teachers might also use checklists like these:

My lessons:

		✓	✗
1.	are fun	☐	☐
2.	arouse curiosity	☐	☐
3.	motivate everyone	☐	☐
4.	are well-planned	☐	☐
5.	fit into a scheme of work	☐	☐
6.	review the previous lesson	☐	☐
7.	use only English	☐	☐
8.	include sufficient tutor-talks	☐	☐
9.	keep up momentum	☐	☐
10.	include child-led routines	☐	☐

The children in my lessons are:

		✓	✗
1.	secure	☐	☐
2.	satisfied	☐	☐
3.	prepared to try and try	☐	☐
4.	enthusiastic	☐	☐
5.	successful	☐	☐
6.	happy speaking English	☐	☐
7.	willing to socialise	☐	☐
8.	happy with their homework	☐	☐

6

Extending spoken ability

6.1 Developing autonomy in the classroom

Before teachers can help lower-primary children they need to understand that the children want to increase their spoken English and are also ready to learn about language. The maturing child is becoming more autonomous, developing his or her own self-learning strategies. These include self-managing strategies to work on projects, and self-analytical strategies which enable the child to look at blocks of language in written form.

To be able to help children in planned lessons or when an impromptu learning opportunity arises, teachers need to be well-prepared. Teaching young children is holistic and demanding, and teachers must be able to respond to children's curiosity and changing needs.

Children have developed their self-learning strategies for acquiring English, but need to constantly renew and broaden them, as autonomy grows. They do this through:

- reviewing the types of language they know and extending their content
- acquiring new types of language to increase their range of use of English (for example, descriptive, coping or emotional language)
- having their phonological awareness of the sounds of English increased, through scaffolding and tutor-talks
- enjoying together their innate desire to play with language.

Children are gradually realising that there is more than one way to say the same thing in English, as in L1. For example, they will learn to use both *I want* ... and *Please can I have* ... . They will enjoy knowing how to say things in a variety of ways. It will make them feel more independent and will motivate them.

6.2 English input

Teachers continue to be children's main English language provider. It is the teacher who orchestrates the use of language within the classroom, but by now children should be able to use language in response to the teacher, and amongst themselves when they are working in pairs or groups. Teachers need to try to make the classroom an all-English room where only English is used. Many teachers are concerned about this, but they have to remember children understand more English than they can use. Children have their own gist-understanding strategies and we should help them to use them in the English classroom. Children watch films in English happily without complaining!

Being able to run an all-English classroom involves careful preparation, as the teacher needs to keep up the English input as well as orchestrating activities, children's responses and use of English throughout. Setting the scene in the first all-English lesson is tiring but it is the way children will use their self-learning strategies and pick up English naturally, and even begin to *think* in English at some point. Inviting an English speaking guest can help!

Types of language:

- Classroom management
- Self language
- Descriptive language
- Socialising language
- Emotional Language
- 'Thinking about thinking' language
- Coping language
- Transactional Language

Too often in an English classroom there are longish pauses when there is no language input. These are wasted opportunities for listening and absorbing language. It is good to compare this situation with the rich language environment created by parents teaching their child to speak L1, where a continuous commentary is given about what is going on around the child. Of course children also need time to reflect, but at this stage of learning these reflection times need to be linked to activities, such as book browsing.

6.2.1 Introducing all-English sessions

Building up all-English experiences and gradually extending them to cover the entire lesson is a method used by some teachers. This can be achieved naturally as a teacher increases his or her own input. However, it is advisable not to tell children that you intend eventually to use only English as this can frighten them. In addition, their parents' reaction to an all-English class can give them unwanted, pre-conceived attitudes. Once these ideas are in children's heads it is difficult to change them.

Children absorb English better if they are not always translating what is said in their head before they react. Teachers can help children not to depend on their own translation by repeating any instructions or information in a natural way, so that children have a second chance to hear the English. Children will get used to this repetition and will wait for it in English. Repetition will diminish quite naturally as children get more used to listening to only English and as they become more fluent in English.

If children reply to the teacher in LI, the teacher should be quick to reflect back what the child has said *in English*. However, the teacher should not discipline children for replying in LI – they may have done so because of lack the ability to say something in English.

Building up using only English takes time. Teachers do not need to worry too much at this stage about cognitive understanding, as many of the cognitive ideas will already have been understood in LI – the child's language of thought. Where cognitive content is new, children generally find links to information they have already learned through LI. Children are used to making connections.

Beginning to introduce all-English sessions is easiest in formal situations where there is a set routine and where children understand what is expected of them. Some teachers have successfully started doing this via a spelling quiz (see Chapter 9, page 185). After quick translations on the first day, the entire activity is only in English. Children who have not completely understood can learn by watching or listening to other children. New spelling words are introduced and practised in context at another time.

Another all-English time used by teachers is tidying-up time. Helping children to develop independence means that they can take more responsibility in the classroom. Initially teachers have to orchestrate the tidying up with management language and a commentary on progress, but eventually the jobs can be handed over to children who will self-manage.

As children gain confidence and use more spoken language, the teacher can increase the number of all-English activities until the classroom becomes all-English. Teachers have to remember that making the transition to using all-English can be difficult and children might need a warming-up period to help make the switch, such as starting the lesson with a short 'Rhyme time' session. The responsibility of organising this can be given to individual or pairs of children who select and orchestrate the session, with the teacher in the background. Selecting rhymes and deciding *who* will say them and *how* is a process, but it also has a product which other children will enjoy making comments about.

6.3 Extending vocabulary

6.3.1 'Show and tell' / 'My secret'

Circle times are important for children as they are all about bringing home to school. At this stage the child-parent-teacher triangle is still very important to the child.

As children get older and more sophisticated, it may be a good idea to change the title of 'Show and tell' to 'My secret'. This tunes in with the child's awareness that he or she is growing up. It also introduces a mystery element to the activity as each child hides his or her 'secret' from classmates until the actual moment when all are gathered to listen to it and see what has been brought in.

'My secret' involves a holistic learning activity in which children have to think about their self-identity. Through their 'secret' they expose their identity to peers, revealing their opinions and values. It is like making a personal statement as it involves thinking about themselves and comparing themselves with others. Critical thinking is involved and time is limited, so children have to consider what is important (what to include), as well as what to leave out.

Parents' support is important as children have to rehearse at home how to speak aloud to others and hold their attention. Even if parents can't speak English they can help their child to practise standing up in front of others and to project his or her voice. Parents like to get involved and want to know how it went, often asking later *How did it go? Did the others like it? What did the teacher say? Were your friends surprised? How did you feel when you showed the class …?*

There are two parts to 'My secret':

1. The process

The child and parents start from the child's 'zone of proximal development' (or 'ZPD' – see Chapter 2, page 41), discussing and deciding what the child will bring to school for 'My secret' and what he or she will say about it. Teachers have to be prepared to co-present the object as some children may need support in using language or may lack the necessary vocabulary. The teacher also needs to be prepared to sum up orally and possibly visually record each child's secret with a photo.

2. The product

The 'My secret' moment includes the satisfaction that comes from talking about real interests, as wells as the motivation that comes from being admired by other children and the teacher. This is particularly the case for boys of primary-school age, who may be reluctant to talk about their real interests with the wider class (especially interests linked to sport or science). It is very important that the teacher supports each child by making sure other children listen fully and understand what is presented.

One teacher recounted the following 'My secret' experience in her lesson:

The boy brought his football-related souvenirs for 'My secret' – including a Chelsea T-shirt and scarf – to tell the class about how he and his dad supported Chelsea. He told everyone the name of his favourite players and adults and children encountered a new side to him. His secret became a talking point for all the boys, as well as some girls, who all began to talk about which football team they or their parents supported. This buzz about football lasted over several lessons.

Organisation

Organising a 'My secret' session is important, especially in large classes where two children presenting may be the maximum in each lesson. Pre-selection of who will present is important as it enables children and families to plan, rehearse and orchestrate the presentation in some way beforehand (the 'process').

Teachers should also be prepared to include their own 'secret', which could be something that introduces new vocabulary naturally, or could be a news flash of some sort (for example, a new baby panda in London Zoo). Teachers should include photos and objects where possible to illustrate their story.

Through 'My secret' teachers can introduce cultural content, comparing it with local culture. This involves children in critical thinking, as well as encouraging them to think about how there are other valid ways of doing the same thing. This increases children's openness to new ideas.

One child recounted the following experience in the lesson:

The teacher talked about her 'secret'. She loves paper. She showed and talked about the range of different qualities of paper made in Japan. The children had a chance to touch, smell and examine paper of different thicknesses, colours and designs. The teacher made a display of many different papers, which parents also enjoyed.

Follow-up

Teachers can add each child's 'My secret' to a class book with text and images, which can become a reference for the classroom book corner. The scrapbook can contain:

- shared writing descriptions of 'My secret' sessions
- photos of the child presenting 'My secret' sessions
- self-assessment by the child (*I liked telling my secret because I could tell the other children about …*)
- reactions of other children (*Ted's secret is a boat he made with his Father. It has an engine and sometimes they sail it on the lake in the park. It's fun to hear about this.*)

The scrapbook can be sent home so parents can read it together with their child. This is very motivating for the child.

6.3.2 Rhyme time

To understand the sounds of English it is important to go on enjoying rhymes, which most children continue to do naturally using their self-language-learning strategies.

'Rhyme time' can be extended beyond rhymes to include other forms of language play, such as jokes. If introduced in a playful way, children will soon pick them up. They can also be made into conversation pieces, passing the reciting from child to child, making the activity an interactive game. Rhymes that include dialogue are fun to use, as children can alter their voice to match each different speaker.

Some classes use story rhymes as the text for their end-of-term concert, although they can of course be used at any time. Although some of the language may seem difficult to transfer, the rhyming nature of the content makes it easier for children to absorb. The experience of learning rhymes and poetry by heart comes easily to children, particularly if they have their own recordings of the pieces. It is a natural way to increase language acquisition.

It is possible to make recordings with English-speaker pa[...]
students. Some recordings can also be found on BBC websites or YouTube.
Listening to recordings whilst doing routine activities at home is a good,
stress-free learning time.

One teacher recounted the following experience:

The school used *The King's Breakfast* by A. A. Milne as their end-of-year
show. The process resulted in all the children and their mothers and
some fathers knowing the whole rhyme by heart before the performance.
No understudies had been prepared but most children knew each
other's roles and acted as prompters, even criticising other children's
performances. In-family English language increased to include *certainly*
(instead of *yes*) and *I'll go and tell … Don't forget …Excuse me … I
didn't really mean it.*

Rhymes

1 **All day long
The sun shines bright.
The moon and stars
Come out by night.**

2 **Said Lizzie,
I'm busy,
I'm building a house.
No hurry,
Don't worry,
Said little Miss Mouse.**

3 **Man fat,
Top hat,
Fell flat,
Squashed hat.**

4   Good better best
    Never stop to rest
    Until your good is better
    And your better is best.

5   (Halloween Rhyme)
    There was a witch lived in a wood,
    When asked her favourite day,
    Gave her questioner a leery grin,
    And cried, 'Why, of course, Flyday!' (Flyday instead
    of Friday)

6   Mary had a little lamb
    Its fleece was black as soot,
    And into Mary's bread and jam
    His sooty foot he put.

7   Blow—wind—blow!
    And go—mill—go!
    That the miller may grind his corn;
    That the baker may take it
    And into bread make it
    And bring us a loaf in the morn. (= morning)

8   If all the world was paper,
    And all the sea was ink,
    If all the trees were bread and cheese,
    What should we have to drink?

9   Apple pie, apple pie,
    Peter likes apple pie.
    So do I, So do I.
    Do you like Apple pie?

10 As I was going out one day
    My head fell off and rolled away.
    But when I saw that it was gone
    I picked it up and put it on.
    And when I got into the street
    A fellow called, 'Look at your feet!'
    I looked at them and sadly said,
    'I left them both asleep in bed!'

11 Seven fat fishermen,
    Sitting side by side,
    Fished from a bridge,
    By the banks of the Clyde.
    The first caught a tiddler,
    The second caught a crab,
    The third caught a winkle,
    The fourth caught a dab. (= a flat fish)
    The fifth caught a tadpole,
    The sixth caught an eel,
    And the seventh, he caught
    An old cartwheel.

12 If you should meet a crocodile,
    Don't take a stick and poke him.
    Ignore the welcome of his smile,
    Be careful not to stroke him.
    For as he sleeps upon the Nile,
    He thinner gets and thinner.
    But when e'er you meet a crocodile,
    He's ready for his dinner!

13 Fidgety Phil
    Will never sit still
    He wriggles
    And giggles
    And then I declare
    He swings backwards
    And forwards
    And tilts
    Up his chair

14 I eat my peas with honey,
    I've done it all my life.
    It makes the peas taste funny,
    But it keeps them on my knife.

15 'Splash' said a raindrop
    As it fell on my hat.
    'Splash' said another
    As it trickled down my back.
    'You are very rude', I said
    As I looked up at the sky.
    Then another raindrop splashed
    Right into my eye.

One-line tongue twisters
1 The sun will surely shine soon.
2 A noisy noise annoys an oyster.
3 The shop that sells short socks shuts soon.
4 This thistle seems like that thistle.

Longer tongue twisters
1 Around the rugged rocks,
   The ragged rascal ran.

2   She sells sea shells by the seashore.
    The shells she sells are sea shells, I'm sure.

3   Swan swam over the sea,
    Swim swan swim.
    Swan swam back again,
    Well swum Swan.

4   I keep six honest serving-men
    (They taught me all I knew);
    Their names are What and Why and When
    And How and Where and Who.
    I send them over land and sea,
    I send them east and west;
    But after they have worked for me,
    I give them all a rest.

Limericks

1   I raised a great hullabaloo (4 syllables)
    When I found a large mouse in my stew.
    Said the waiter, 'Don't shout
    And wave it about,
    Or the rest will be wanting one, too!'

2   A sea-serpent saw a big tanker,
    Bit a hole in her side and then sank her.
    It swallowed the crew
    In a minute or two,
    And then picked its teeth with the anchor.

3   I sat next to the duchess at tea,
    It was just as I feared it would be.
    Her rumblings abdominal
    Were simply phenomenal,
    And everyone thought it was me!

4 There was young man from Dundee
Who climbed a very high tree.
He felt such a clown,
He couldn't get down.
He's been there since 1903. (pronounced 'nineteen oh three')

5 There was a young man called Fred
Who always slept under the bed.
Said his friends, 'Oh, how strange!
It's time for a change.'
So he sleeps 'neath the bookcase instead.

Rhymes for starting games
I Red, white and blue,
The cat's got the flu.
The baby has the whooping cough
And out goes YOU.

2 Inky, pinky, ponky,
My Daddy bought a donkey.
The donkey died,
Daddy cried,
Inky, pinky, ponky.
Out goes you.

Fun with numbers

Playing with numbers is a fast way to increase the use of English, and is quickly understood once children have learned to use the new names for numbers in English.

Q: *What did 9 say to 6?*
A: *You're upside down.*

Q: *Look at 1961. Do you know another number which stays the same upside down?*
A: *1881.*

Q: *What has six legs, four ears and a tail?*
A: *A man on a horse!*

Fun with words (jokes)

Playing with words is something children do naturally and it is easy to build on this as it increases phonological knowledge as well as fluency.

Q: *What keys cannot turn locks?*
A: *Monkeys and donkeys!*

Q: *What's green and jumps around the garden?*
A: *A spring onion!*

Q: *What stays hot in the fridge?*
A: *Mustard!*

Q: *Why does the pony cough?*
A: *He is a little hoarse!*

Q: *Why should you take a ruler to bed with you?*
A: *To see how long you sleep!*

Q: *What kind of dog has no tail?*
A: *A hot dog!*

Q: *Which tables can we eat?*
A: *Vegetables!*

Q: *Who says 'Oh! Oh! Oh!' ?*
A: *Santa walking backwards!* (Santa usually says 'Ho! Ho! Ho!')

Q: *What grows in a field and makes music?*
A: *Pop corn!*

Q: *What do frogs drink?*
A: *Croak-a-cola!*

Q: *What is the biggest moth?*
A: *A Mammoth!*

Q: *What do you call two banana peels on the floor?*
A: *Slippers!*

Q: *Which animal can you never trust?*
A: *A cheetah because he cheats you.*

Q: *Where do tadpoles change into frogs?*
A: *In the croakroom!* (instead of 'cloakroom')

Q: *Why do bees hum?*
A: *Because they have forgotten the words!*

Q: *What did the biscuits say to the peanuts?*
A: *You're nuts and we're crackers!* ('crackers' and 'nuts' both mean silly)

Q: *How do you keep cool at a football match?*
A: *Stand by a fan!* (A 'fan' is someone who likes football, and a machine to blow cold air on you.)

Q: *Why does a giraffe have a long neck?*
A: *Because his head is so far from his body.*

Q: *What goes out but never comes in?*
A: *A fire!*

'Knock Knock' jokes

These can be recited as mini-conversations between two children.

1   **Knock, knock.**
    Who's there?
    Canoe.
    Canoe who?
    Canoe help me with my homework? (instead of 'Can you')

2   **Knock, knock.**
    Who's there?
    Police.
    Police who?
    Police hurry up. It's chilly outside! (instead of 'Please')

3   **Knock, knock.**
    Who's there?
    Cows.
    Cows who?
    Cows don't go 'who', they go 'moo'!

4   **Knock, knock.**
    Who's there?
    Cook.
    Cook who.
    I know you are! ('cuckoo' also means 'silly')

Back-to-front words

was	saw	pots	stop
trap	part	loop	pool

Super duper chants (three voices)

Voice one	Voice two	Voice three
high	higher than	the HIGHEST
tall	taller than	the TALLEST
small	smaller than	the SMALLEST
big	bigger than	the BIGGEST
beautiful	more beautiful than	the MOST beautiful
helpful	more helpful than	the MOST helpful
good	better than	the BEST
bad	worse than	the WORST

Children's natural ability to pick up language is often regarded as a chore by parents. However, it is a natural skill that needs stoking, as without practice it gets rusty and with age more difficult to retrieve.

> What is acquired through play is not specific information but a general (mind)set towards solving problems that includes both abstraction and combinatorial flexibility [where children] string bits of behaviour together to form novel solutions to problems requiring the restructuring of thought or action.
>
> (Sylva)

7

Introducing reading English

7.1 Reading as a skill

Reading is more than word recognition – it is arguably the single most important skill anyone will have to learn in life. Written language has to be interpreted without either the writer or a mediator being present. However, readers only have to learn the mechanics of reading once in a lifetime; once the strategies of how to decode to get meaning from text have been acquired, they can be applied to decode content in other languages.

Young children enjoy playing with language – they do it naturally, initiating it themselves. Teachers need to harness their innate play-like language practices and use them to aid the acquisition of language. This means teachers need to think about how they present English and English literacy. It is possible for children to absorb imposed phonic rules, but teacher-led academic analysis is not the way most young children enjoy learning at this age. It can blunt some children's enthusiasm for activities that accompany book reading.

7.1.1 Young readers

Most young children around 7 years of age are already readers. They will have started to read in LI and thus understand the mechanical process of reading, as well as any LI content. Knowledge of the mechanics of reading can be easily transferred to their English reading, leaving only the decoding of the new English content.

It is astonishing how children manage to decode texts and get meaning at such a young age. For the young child, decoding text includes:

- working out how to read the words aloud, and later silently
- thinking about the meaning of known and unknown words
- fitting the words together to make meaning of the whole text
- using context clues from illustrations or photographs, linking these clues to meanings in past experiences and previous texts
- using different eye-hand movements (for those who are learning to decode a new script).

Recent research in neuroscience makes it clear that the human brain now develops much sooner than was believed by Jean Piaget and other well-known researchers of the mid-twentieth century. It is clear that early stimulation is proving to be highly effective in young children's brain development, making them capable of forming strategies at an earlier age than was previously thought (see Chapter 2, page 32).

Many young readers may now be able to recognise patterns and make analogies between the new and known sooner than children could twenty or thirty years ago. This can partly be explained by early visual exposure to content on screens, and by engagement with interactive activities which children experience as soon as they can swipe a tablet.

With the spread of technology, more young children will hear some English from a very early age. They will even see examples of the Roman alphabet on screens and in their environment, which – if their own writing script is different – will be a new visual experience. Many will have travelled the world 'on screen', and 'visited' other countries. They may be able to recite the names of pop stars, actors and sports personalities. The world has come to them, and adults may be surprised by children's wide general knowledge!

7.1.2 Reading in English

Reading in two languages plays a significant contribution in developing higher levels of cognitive functioning.

(Harding and Riley)

Reading in English entails fitting 44 sounds into the 26 letters of the Roman alphabet, meaning there are fewer one-to-one matches of sound and symbol than in some other languages written in Roman letters (like French, Spanish, Italian, Indonesian and Malaysian – children with such languages as L1 often learn to read amazingly quickly).

Young children whose language is not encoded in Roman letters (for example, Arabic, Thai, Japanese or Chinese) first have to be taught the Roman alphabet (see Chapter 8, page 168). As Arabic is written from

113

right to left, and most Japanese primary school textbooks from the top to the bottom of the page, this also involves getting used to the different eye movements needed for reading English. Although this additional learning takes time, young children, unlike some adults, often take it in their stride. Young children at this age are learning new things and adapting to them all the time. Some may even be learning another new form of reading simultaneously (for example, learning to read music to play an instrument).

If young readers are to progress quickly and remain motivated, they need to be exposed to varied, interesting written English experiences. They will soon discover they can reuse and build on their existing LI strategies to decode English. They know how to use cues to decode text, and when to make a guess from experiences in reading LI. Teachers need to let the child experiment, rather than imposing rules or a different way of decoding.

Many LI readers may have already begun to analyse the patterns in English words they recognise. LI readers, if they have a good oral base in English, soon move on from reading English word by word to reading whole phrases. If they have a good model in the teacher, they often read from the beginning with good pronunciation and meaningful intonation, including enjoying using stress to add interest to what they are reading. They might particularly enjoy adding accents, mood, attitudes and emotions to a story when reading direct speech. To read books (and visual exposures on screen) they will be using multi-decoding strategies, which teachers may find difficult to assess.

To effectively teach young children all the sounds of English using only a synthetic phonics programme is not an easy task, even for native-English-speaker teachers and parents. This is because many adults did not learn to read by the synthetic phonic method themselves. Furthermore, little detailed advice is available for parents, so teachers need to keep parents regularly informed about the children's 'learning to read' activities. If teachers do not offer parents this kind of support, they may look for added support on the Internet which may add confusion due to the prevalence of texts not edited by professionals in the phonic sounds of English (see Chapter 2, page 32).

If teachers are to help young children transfer their different self-decoding strategies to read English, it is wise not to impose a single teacher-led phonic decoding method. Children should instead be provided with diverse activities that enable them to work out by themselves how to transfer and reuse their multi-strategies to decode. Children are self-educators and learn by doing.

The choice of activities needs to be flexible, responding to the children's 'zone of proximal development' ('ZPD' – see Chapter 2, page 41), interests and needs. Where necessary, explanatory tutor-talks should be included, following a structured hidden syllabus (see Chapter 5, page 82). Through these focused tutor-talks, the teacher can introduce the basic sound–letter relationships and discuss them in interesting, playful ways that motivate (see Chapter 1, page 19 – the Playful Approach).

Young children need support and encouragement from the teacher in the initial stages of transfer and reuse of decoding strategies, as it takes time and effort. Progress depends on children's oral foundation, and care needs to be taken that, in their eagerness to read, readers do not resort to using the sounds of L1 to decode, thus reading English with a foreign accent. Once children get into the habit of reading English with their L1 decoding sounds, it takes volition and perseverance on the part of the child to self-correct their habit.

Self-teaching English sound patterns and linking them (making analogies) to their own experiences is what children innately know and want to do. As they become aware of their own progress, they become more confident. Self-motivated learning is likely to be deeper and more long-lasting than teacher-imposed phonic rules.

Young L1 readers come to their first English lessons with an innate drive to learn to read in English, as reading and writing is what they and their families expect; it is seen as a sign and measure of progress and growing up. Being able to read aloud to an audience can give children confidence and motivates them. For this reason, teachers should consider preparing with them special 'show off' pieces, such as reciting known rhymes or playing games involving reading (see Chapter 9, page 196), that can act as 'proof' of learning to the child's family.

Although some children seem to decode English words easily, it is better not to expose them to stories with too many new words until they have consolidated and increased their reading ability. Some children may find reading English difficult, but they can be motivated to persevere if it is presented as a challenge, similar to cracking a 'secret' code.

Once children have transferred their reading strategies to English, their progress appears to be linked to their ability to read in L1. Children who are good readers in L1 also seem to quickly become good readers in English. Conversely, children who have reading difficulties in L1 often have similar difficulties in reading English. However, in cases where a child's reading difficulties are linked to emotional well-being, these problems may not be transferred to English and the child may become a better reader in English than in L1.

7.1.3 Teaching children to read English

Many non-native-English speakers are surprised to hear that for some native-English-speaker children learning to read is not easy, and that to reach fluency generally takes a minimum of two years. Although the UK government recommends learning to read through synthetic phonics migrants to the UK are amazed that there is no one textbook used by every UK state school for teaching this method of reading.

Learning to decode letters and learning to encode letters are intrinsically interlinked; therefore learning to spell and spelling quizzes should support reading (see Chapter 9, page 185). Discussion continues as to which skill should be taught first, however. Children who want to write before they have learned handwriting should be encouraged to do so using a 'moveable alphabet'. This could be made of letter shapes in wood or plastic, used with or without a white board. As English is a vowel-rich language, moveable alphabet packs need extra vowel letters (*a e i o u* and *y*) if children are to be able to write several words or phrases.

To learn to read using synthetic phonics, native-English-speaker children need to:

- have good oral ability
- have been exposed to a 'ready-to-read' programme
- follow a graded set of books (a reading scheme) introducing a structured synthetic phonics programme, based on the difficulty of decoding words rather than meaning (which is conveyed through supportive illustrations)
- be living in a society where some English is used, in order to get meaning from the words selected to fit the sound pattern they are learning to decode (synthetic phonics teaches how to build up and blend sounds to make a whole word, for example, *p-e-g ... s-ai-d ... br-ea-d*)
- have teachers who are knowledgeable about phonics and who can introduce the sounds of English in interesting, memorable ways
- have teachers who can inform parents about the phonic rules and exceptions. (Many parents, even native-English speakers, find it difficult to link sounds to letters. For example, a parent might make the mistake of having their child sound out the separate sounds *t, h* and *e* in the word *the*, not realising that *the* should be learned as a whole word by sight recognition because the diagraph *th* cannot be learned by sounding out its individual letters.)

7.1.4 Reading strategies

Some children come to school already reading simple L1 texts, having been shown how to decode by their parents, siblings or grandparents at home. This is often the case with younger children where parents have read picture books to them in a phonetic-based L1, in which most of the letters match the sounds (as in Italian, Spanish, Indonesian and Malay, for example).

Young readers in LI are unique and difficult to assess. However, teachers can understand something about their decoding strategies by finding out how they were taught to read in LI. Readers who come from a non-Roman-alphabet LI background may have some different or more developed strategies than children who do have a Roman-alphabet LI. This can be the case for Chinese children, whose sight recognition may be more precise since the misplacement of one dot, or the addition of one extra stroke, can entirely change the meaning of a Chinese character.

> *Most teachers are unlikely to believe that there is only one way to teach reading that will work for every child. This is because reading is a very complicated mix of thinking skills and experience.*
>
> (Whitehead)

Most LI readers learning English will already have developed their own effective multi-strategies for decoding LI text. When this is the case, no single method of learning to read English will use all their strategies and satisfy their feeling of being a reader. Teachers soon find out that using only the synthetic phonic method of learning to read English is not suitable for young LI readers who:

- have already developed their self-decoding strategies and expect to use them to read quickly and to the same standard as they read in LI
- have a limited oral foundation (as they are living in a non-English-speaking society) and therefore find some of the words/phrases included for their sound/letter combination difficult to decode/understand.

To take LI readers back to the first rules of a phonic reading scheme with simple language content can be boring and demotivating. Young readers expect to transfer and reuse their already-existing reading strategies immediately and effectively when they start to read in English.

Decoding strategy clues for Roman alphabets

Shape of the word

- Length
- Letters above or below the base line
- Initial and/or final letter
- Letter pattern within the word

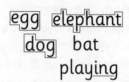

Sound of the word

- Onset (first letter, consonant or consonant blend in a word): **m**/ouse, **sh**/ip (see page 137)
- Rime (old form of the word *rhyme*), based on the letter/sound pattern after the onset: c/**ake**, b/**ake** (see page 137)
- Analysis based on letter/sound knowledge of the content of a word (analytic phonics)
- The sound of the word is worked out and possibly related to the previous oral experience using analogy strategies (analogy phonics)
- Word families: *beautiful/beauty, sing/singer/song*
- Words within words (compound words): *sun/set, foot/ball, air/port*
- Alliteration: **s**he **s**aw **s**even **s**wans **s**wimming on the **s**outh **s**ea
- Position of the word in the structure (phrase or sentence)
- Prediction of unrecognised word meaning from previous use of spoken language

Context

- Information obtained from the text gives clues to meanings of unrecognised word

Images

- Illustrations and photographs offer clues to meaning

7.2 A multi-strategy English reading scheme

Most L1 readers are flexible and quick to unconsciously adapt their decoding strategies to reuse them in a multi-strategy reading scheme. Classroom teachers may think about teaching one method of learning to read, but children think holistically. They know how to read and want to try and find out, for themselves, how to read English. Teachers need to provide children with a variety of enabling, motivating experiences that help them to help themselves.

> *Learning phonics can never be more than a part of learning to read.*

> (Dombey)

Although both synthetic phonics and analytic phonics are essential components of early reading, they are only part of the many self-learning strategies young readers may already use.

A multi-strategy reading scheme of English is closely intertwined with a learning-to-spell scheme. Spelling quizzes support words that children are learning to read. Both schemes build on from young children's zone of proximal development (ZPD) and self-reading strategies, respecting that they are already readers in L1.

A multi-strategy reading scheme helps L1 readers:

- transfer and reuse self-learning strategies by providing enabling, easy-to-do activities
- adapt self-learning strategies to English and develop phonological awareness skills in English (getting used to hearing sounds, syllables and words and talking about them)
- develop new strategies for decoding known spoken English in written form
- look for patterns in known spoken English, including rhymes, alliteration, word plays, word families and compound words
- increase their bank of words to break into syllables (see Chapter 9, Spelling).

*It is accepted that children do not need to know the 166
rules or more plus the 45 exceptions before they can read
well. We know that children with a reliable basis can puzzle
out words that follow rules they haven't been taught.*

(Dombey)

Once readers have acquired a certain amount of knowledge and feel confident about how to reuse their self-decoding strategies, they begin to teach themselves to read and, by themselves, they begin to explore new texts. Teachers need to try to assess children's own strategies and build on them, using them as a starting point in helping children to effectively reuse their self-decoding strategies and get results. Teachers should be prepared to mix-and-match, drawing on a bank of supportive, new experiences in which children can try out their self-decoding strategies.

7.2.1 The alphabet

For non-Roman-alphabet readers, reading English starts a step earlier as children need first to be able to use both the names and the sounds of the letters of the alphabet for talking about all forms of literacy (see Chapter 9, page 178).

Games can be used to consolidate alphabet letter names and sounds, which will appeal to children who may feel learning the alphabet is 'babyish'. Readers often enjoy singing the alphabet song in pairs or groups, matching capitals to small letter cards as they sing. Children can do the same for homework, listening to ABC recordings on YouTube, gradually speeding up the game to match the recorded song.

7.2.2 Whole-word sight recognition

In literate societies and societies where there is easy access to screen and hand-held technology, most children learn to recognise their own name in English, as well as the names of English logos for things like confectionery, famous drink brands or types of car. This happens almost unaided and from a very young age.

Collecting environmental words already known in English and that can be read by sight recognition as a 'block' (Gestalt) can be made into a fun experience. Young children are often proud to see how much English they already know and can read. Getting parents involved adds to the fun as they, too, may be surprised to see how much English is actually used in everyday life.

Through shared reading with adults, children may also already 'read' words like *No* or *Exit* using the strategy referred to as 'Look and Say'. Children recognise whole words without realising that they are 'reading' a block of letters that make up a word. If a text is already known orally and children have been introduced to new words on cards in a game, they can read the words using this 'Look and Say' strategy.

Figure 3 Recognising whole words

Once early readers have seen a written word approximately five times (the number depends on a child's maturity, focus and self-reading strategies), most can recognise and read it by themselves without having to decode it aloud, letter by letter, or being told how to read it. Some readers, who have acquired sight recognition of about fifty English words, begin to develop their own self-decoding strategies and start reading simple texts by themselves, probably reusing other strategies. Provided these children's efforts are encouraged and they are given plenty of short, well-selected reading texts, they progress rapidly to become confident decoders (readers).

Many teachers have found it successful to begin teaching to read English by building on children's existing ability to recognise whole words by sight. This early success motivates and gives readers confidence to tackle the problems they later encounter on the way to becoming fluent decoders of English.

7.2.3 High-frequency words

Although patterns are inconsistent, it is said that when English spelling rules take into account syllable structure, phonetics and accents, the rules are more than 75% reliable.

Some words like *the, a, he, are,* in which only part can be decoded, are referred to by adults for convenience as 'puzzle words', 'tricky words' or 'key words'. When children get stuck at one of these words in the initial stages of learning to read, adults might say *Try again … it's a puzzle word.* This implies that the child should try a different strategy, for example trying to read the word as a whole word ('Look and Say') by getting clues from the parts of the word that can be decoded. For example, in the word *all* the child might recognise the double *l* seen previously in the word *ball.*

When writing texts teachers often find it necessary to include a few 'puzzle words' to make meaning and to attract children's interests. Some teachers add fun words to insert a playful approach.

Figure 4 High-frequency words

100 high-frequency words in order

1. the	21. that	41. not	61. look	81. put
2. and	22. with	42. then	62. don't	82. could
3. a	23. all	43. were	63. come	83. house
4. to	24. we	44. go	64. will	84. old
5. said	25. can	45. little	65. into	85. too
6. in	26. are	46. as	66. back	86. by
7. he	27. up	47. no	67. from	87. day
8. I	28. had	48. mum	68. children	88. made
9. of	29. my	49. one	69. him	89. time
10. it	30. her	50. them	70. Mr	90. I'm
11. was	31. what	51. do	71. get	91. if
12. you	32. there	52. me	72. just	92. help
13. they	33. out	53. down	73. now	93. Mrs
14. on	34. this	54. dad	74. came	94. called
15. she	35. have	55. big	75. oh	95. here
16. is	36. went	56. when	76. about	96. off
17. for	37. be	57. it's	77. got	97. asked
18. at	38. like	58. see	78. their	98. saw
19. his	39. some	59. looked	79. people	99. make
20. but	40. so	60. very	80. your	100. an

(Table from Masterson, J., Stuart, M., Dixon, M. and Lovejoy, S. (2003) Children's Printed Word Database: Economic and Social Research Council funded project, R00023406)

For the next 200 common words, please see the Appendix (pages 238–239).

These 12 words make up a quarter of what children read and write:

a   and   he   I   is   in   of   it   the   that   was   to

The 20 next most frequent words are:

all   as   at   be   but   are   for   had   have   him
his   not   on   one   said   so   they   we   with   you

7.2.4 Using word cards

A large number of cards are needed for teaching and playing games. Teachers can easily print their own cards, using a font that resembles as closely as possible the font in first reading books. Black print on light-coloured, thick paper or thin card is best, as the print shows up clearly. It should be remembered that any uneven space between letters/words and any poorly shaped letters can be confusing for children in the initial stages of learning. If printed letters are sometimes different from handwriting (as in the letters *a/a* and *g/g*), explanations showing both are needed. Children soon manage to recognise both without difficulty.

The puzzle word game

- The teacher creates four cards for each of the 'puzzle words' he or she is teaching. The cards are placed face down in a pack, in any order.
- The teacher picks up the first card, holds it up and says *Read this. What does it say?*.
- The first child to read the word correctly keeps the card.
- The teacher then picks up the second card and the game continues in the same way until all the cards are used.
- The teacher then asks the children *How many cards have you got?*. In turn, they count their cards aloud saying *One, two, three*, etc. The winner is the child with the most cards.
- The teacher then collects the cards, asking first for all the cards with puzzle word 1, then for all the cards with puzzle word 2, etc.
- The game can be adapted as children learn more words and additional word cards can be added to the pack. When the pack gets too big, the teacher keeps the words that need the most consolidation and discards the others.

Children also enjoy having their own mini-cards, made with a font size of between 8mm and 10mm high. Mini-cards be used:

- to play games in groups
- to match with words in texts
- to build rhymes
- as cards in games like *What's this? Snap, Bingo* etc.

Mini-cards are very useful as they give children an opportunity to work at their own speed, thinking about how and what they are doing. Children need time to reflect when reading, as it is during this time that they work out and adapt their self-strategies for decoding. For this reason it is essential to ensure that they are not exposed *only* to mini-card work that demands quick responses. Individual work with mini-cards also gives teachers an opportunity to check that children are not guessing words and really know how to read them.

As soon as children can recognise the lower case letters of the alphabet, mini-cards of up to four whole words per lesson can be introduced. As their sight recognition of words expands, the number can be increased. The same method of introduction as for alphabet letters can be used, but since the word is read the adult or child's hand should move from left to right to indicate the way of writing the word. It is useful to let children go over their cards in pairs a second time later in a lesson, if time allows, as this helps in learning.

Mini-cards can also be used for words included in spelling activities (see Chapter 9, page 179), until children have built up a reading vocabulary of over fifty words. By that time, most readers have reused sufficient self-strategies to read words they already know orally. In all cases, mini-cards should only be used for words children already know orally.

Mini-card game

This game is useful to support reading Consonant-Vowel-Consonant (CVC) words. It can be played individually, in pairs, in small groups or with the whole class.

Set 1:

Make mini-cards for:

Letters: *b   c   f   h   m   p   r   s*

Words: *bat   cat   fat   hat   mat   pat   rat   sat*

The teacher deals out the cards to the group, pair or class.

The teacher calls out the alphabet letter names in order: *a,b,c,d,e,f,* etc. The child who has the letter *b* holds it up and says *b*.

The teacher then asks *Has any one got a word beginning with b?*

The child who has the card *bat* holds it up and says *I have.*

The card with the word *bat* is put in the middle of the circle/table and the card with the letter *b* is placed next to it.

The game continues until the teacher has said the complete alphabet. Play again using other sets of cards, for example:

Set 2:

Letters: *b   r   l   s   p   p*   (2 × letter *p*)

Words: *bed   red   leg   set   peg   pet*

Set 3:

Letters: *b   f   h   l   t   s   s*   (2 × letter *s*)

Words: *bit   fit   hit   lip   tip   sit   sip*

Set 4:

Letters: *c   r   s   m   m   p   p   p*   (2 × letter *m*; 3 × letter *p*)

Word: *can   ran   sad   mad   man   pan   pod   pad*

Figure 5 Classroom labels

It is also very useful to make classroom labels for new words (these can be put on actual objects or on pictures of objects). A typical English classroom will be full of such labels, which children probably read mostly by sight recognition. Pictures need to be clearly labelled and changed regularly, as after a certain time children stop reading over-familiar labels.

Introduce a daily word and talk with the children about 'today's new word'. Each new word can be emailed to parents in a form that can be printed out and stuck into a special word book, or placed around the home for children to see.

7.2.5 Reading and 'writing' rhymes

An articulate child familiar with words will read more easily because words are already in his head.

(Garfield)

The 'reading' (whole-word recognition) of simple, short rhymes children already know orally is an important step in learning to read. Matching known oral language with written language gives children a feeling they can 'read' and builds up confidence.

When children have been introduced to cards of all the words in a particular rhyme they already know orally, they can arrange the cards on the floor to 'write' the rhyme. As the cards are placed, the class can talk about reading strategies such as onset, rime and puzzle words.

Having 'written' the rhyme using the cards, and having read the rhyme aloud, children can then be given the text in a rhyme book. As they know the rhyme orally, they quickly pass from reading word by word to reading phrases and whole lines with correct stress and intonation. To their surprise they discover they can read straight away! Children who have learned to 'read' three or four rhymes this way often have the confidence to then teach themselves to read other simple rhymes they know orally.

Figure 6 Writing a rhyme with cards

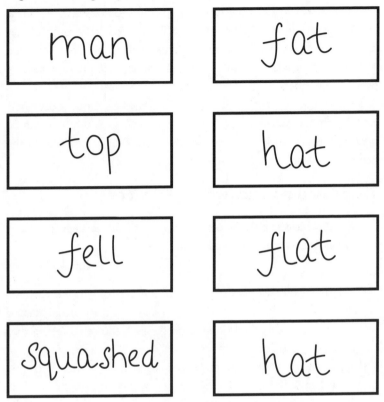

The written 'code' is what we are asking children to learn to read. It's a code that they don't use when speaking with family and friends.

(Rosen)

How to make a rhyme book

The teacher prints and distributes rhymes that have been 'written' in class to the children.

For homework, the children stick their printed rhymes into a scrapbook called *My Rhyme Book* and add illustrations of their own. The rhyme sheets may be for reading practice or they can be used to copy for handwriting practice.

Some children are excited to find that they can successfully self-dictate the rhymes as they know them already by heart (see Chapter 6, page 101, Rhyme 3).

7.3 Finding out about words

Early reading is supported by spelling and conversely spelling is supported by reading texts; the two are intertwined (see Chapter 9, page 178). Tutor-talks about spelling patterns and words give added support.

Learning a language and learning *about* a language are different. As children begin to copy and create text, they begin to learn about the role of words to make meaning. Children's questions about language, as they read and create text, indicate that they are ready to be introduced to basic grammar through focused tutor-talks.

7.3.1 Syllables

Syllables are made up of phonemes and are the phonological building blocks of words. Syllables help children become aware of the sequences of sounds in words (see Chapter 9, page 187).

All words have syllables, even if some have only one! Syllables are more important than is often realised in learning to read and spell. Breaking words into speech sounds (syllables) is something young children and their parents can easily understand as they may do it already in L1, without realising it. Children and adults can sometimes be heard in a monologue breaking down long words aloud as a self-help strategy, as they try to read or spell them.

One syllable: *big, small, wrong, right, day, night, high, low, foot, toe, bad*
Two syllables: *lu/cky, fun/ny, se/ven, thir/teen, twen/ty, plen/ty, to/day*
Three syllables: *un/lu/cky, ham/bur/ger, di/no/saur, e/le/ven, se/ven/teen*
Four syllables: *wa/ter/me/lon, ca/ter/pil/lar, he/li/cop/ter, al/li/ga/tor*

Playing with syllables can be fun and interesting, too! Tutor-talks can explain how words are made of syllables and how how to play with syllables. Children sometimes like to play using a robot-like voice to say each syllable in a word!

Blend: where consecutive letters are pronounced with a single identity
(**bl**/*ack*, **tr**/*ain*, **spr**/*ing*)
Diagraph: where two letters represent one sound (*sh, ch, th, wh, ph*)
Diphthong: where a sound is comprised of one vowel sound gliding into another (*ou* in *loud*; *ai* in *rain*; *oy* in *toy*)

7.3.2 Little books

Building on children's self-strategy to use the whole-word or 'Look and Say' approach, teachers can guide children to read simple books. This is what children really want to do as it represents 'real reading' for them.

Planning an early 'real reading' experience motivates and gives children confidence. Teachers need to plan carefully to include successes in a multi-strategy learning-to-read scheme (even in reading games), as any failure in these initial stages can demotivate and be difficult to reverse, with children saying things like *I can't read English. It is too difficult for me. My parents say English is difficult.*

By introducing three-letter words (consonant, short vowel, consonant), children progress quickly to reading simple texts in short books. Most three- or four-letter words are simple to decode and children soon pass from blending aloud (/h-a-t/) to looking and then saying the whole word.

Little books aim to give:

- first 'real reading' experiences in English
- positive feelings about reading English
- motivation to self-direct effort to reuse reading strategies (especially important for boys, who are sometimes later readers than girls)
- fun reading experiences, that make children think!

Level 1 books contain:
three-letter words
single letters to blend (/m-a-n/)
puzzle words

Level 2 books contain:
diagraphs or blends
patterns
puzzle words

In order not to confuse or discourage at this stage of learning to read, it is better to leave until later explanations about initial alphabet letters that can be pronounced in two different ways, like /c/ in cat and /c/ in city. Explain this instead when making a 'First dictionary' (see Chapter 11, page 222).

This building up of letters to make words (synthetic phonics) to read at this stage in a multi-strategy scheme gives immediate success and thus motivates. However, the experience is limiting as blending letters does not train the eye to see a whole word. Furthermore, short texts comprised of easy-to-decode words give little experience of how the position of a word in a sentence gives meaning. The arrangement of words for meaning in a sentence in L1 may differ from English. Adult language learners often find word order more confusing than young children, who rarely make mistakes.

How to make little books

The teacher makes an eight-page mini-book for each child by cutting a sheet of A4 paper into four quarters. The four pieces are then stacked and stapled across the middle to make the booklets.

Figure 7 Little Books

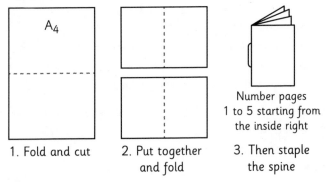

1. Fold and cut

2. Put together and fold

Number pages 1 to 5 starting from the inside right

3. Then staple the spine

The teacher prints out the story text, using a font which matches reading text or handwriting style, and making sure words are spaced out for easier reading.

Children are helped to glue the story text into their little book. As the text is stuck into the books, the children and/or teacher can read the text aloud, pointing to each word.

Children can illustrate their stories themselves or – if they are less confident – colour in an illustration. Alternatively, they can cut out pictures from comics or magazines to decorate their little book.

After making their first little books, the children might like to continue making others. Sometimes children enthusiastically fill in their own little books at home if teachers make blank ones available.

Figure 8 Storyboard for a mini-book

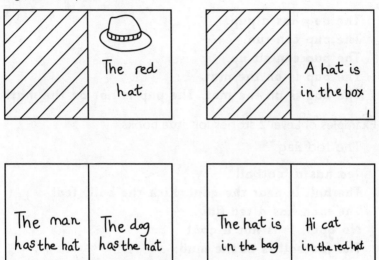

Examples of Level I stories for little books

The sad dog

**The man has a fat dog.
The dog is sad.
The dog has a bad leg.
The dog cannot beg.
Pat the dog!**

No, dog, no!

**Ted is in bed.
Ted has a bad leg.
His dog is sad.
His dog is on the bed.
Bad dog! Not on the bed.**

The dog and the pup

The dog has a pup.
The pup can run.
The pup can sit up.
The pup is on the mat.
The dog is on the mat. The pup is not on the mat!

Examples of Level 2 stories for little books

The red flag

Ted has a football.
The ball is near the goal. Kick the ball, Ted!
The man has a red flag.
No goal. It is not a goal.
The football is in the mud.

The lift

A cat is in the lift
The lift can go up.
The lift can go up, up, up to the top.
The lift stops.
The cat is glad. It can get out.

7.3.3 Onset and rime

Patterning of Onset and Rimes make up a substantial part of patterning of English spelling. Once we start to see words this way, our sense that English spelling is chaotic is much reduced.

(Dombey)

'Onset and rime' is a technical term used to describe two units which make up a spoken syllable. The initial unit, 'onset', is made up of a single consonant (*d* in *d/og*) or a blend of two or more consonants (*sh* in *sh/ip*; *str* in *str/ing*). The second unit, 'rime', begins from the first vowel after the onset (*og* in *d/og*; *ip* in *sh/ip*).

Rime units are always pronounceable on their own and provide a more reliable guide to spelling. They break down a word to make recognising patterns easier. Rime patterns in their simplest form look and sound alike (*h/at*, *c/at*, *m/at*, *th/at*). However, they can look alike but sound different, for example *read* (present tense) and *read* (past tense). They can also look different but sound alike, for example *bear* and *bare* or *grate and great*.

Rhyming words have the same rimes but with changing onset consonants or consonant blends: *c/at*, *s/at*, *m/at*, *fl/at* (Goswani and Bryant 1990).

Children enjoy playing with rhyming words and have a natural ability to pick up rhymes. Their enjoyment of playing with sounds means that many have, in fact, already played with onset and rime during games, changing the consonant (onset) but using the same sounding rhymes (rimes): *c/ake*, *b/ake*, *m/ake*, *t/ake*.

Building on young children's previously acquired self-learning strategies, playing with alliteration and rhyming is a natural way to introduce the concept of breaking words down into units smaller than a syllable. Research has shown (Wise, Olson and Treimain 1990) that children are more successful at decoding words divided by onset and rime than by using any other type of division, so teachers can help children recognise patterns by introducing words in this way.

Children use onset and rime to make analogies between known and unknown words.

(Goswami and Bryant)

Common rimes

/ack	sack back	/ip	lip ship
/ag	bag rag	/it	bit sit
/an	can ran	/ix	six mix
/all	ball fall (ll as one sound)	/ock	sock rock (ck as one sound)
/at	bat cat	/og	dog fog
/ed	bed red	/op	top pop
/eg	leg peg	/ot	hot pot
/ell	bell tell	/ox	fox box (also socks clocks)
/en	ten pen	/uff	puff (ff as one sound)
/ig	big pig	/ug	bug jug
/ill	hill (ll as one sound)	/un	sun run
/in	bin pin	/ut	hut but
/ing	ring king	/uzz	buzz fuzz (zz as one sound)

Two syllable words can be divided in the same way
cl/ever, n/ever; t/umble, m/umble

Figure 9 The 37 rimes which make up nearly 500 words

-ack	-ain	-ake	-ale
-all	-ame	-an	-ank
-ap	-ash	-at	-ate
-aw	-ay	eat	-ell
-est	-ice	-ick	-ide
-ite	-ill	-in	-ine
-ing	-ink	-ip	-ir
-ock	-oke	-op	-or
-ore	-uck	-ug	-ump
-unk			
(Wylie and Durell, 1970)			

Figure 10 37 Basic phonograms

Rime	Examples
-ack	back, black, crack, Jack, Mack, sack, Shack, stack, tack, track, rack, pack, whack, Zack
-ail	fail, frail, Gail, hail, jail, mail, nail, pail, quail, rail, sail, tail, trail, wail
-ain	brain, drain, Cain, chain, gain, grain, main, pain, plain, rain, stain, strain, train
-ake	bake, Blake, brake, cake, fake, Jake, lake, make, rake, sake, shake, stake, take, wake
-ale	ale, bale, Dale, Gale, male, pale, sale, stale, tale, whale
-ame	blame, came, dame, fame, flame, game, lame, name, same, shame, tame
-an	an, ban, can, Dan, fan, Fran, Jan, man, Nan, pan, plan, ran, Stan, tan, than, van
-ank	bank, blank, clank, Frank, Hank, sank, tank, thank, yank
-ap	cap, chap, clap, crap, flap, lap, map, nap, rap, sap, slap, strap, tap, trap, wrap, zap
-ash	ash, bash, cash, clash, crash, dash, flash, gash, lash, mash, rash, sash, splash, stash
-at	At, bat, brat, cat, fat, flat hat, mat, pat, rat, sat, splat, stat, that
-ate	ate, crate, gate, grate, hate, late, mate, Nate, plate, rate, slate, state
-aw	caw, claw, draw, flaw, jaw, law, paw, saw, straw,
-ay	bay, clay, day, gray, hay, Jay, lay, may, pay, play, pray, say, slay, stay, stray, way
-eat	beat, bleat, cheat, cleat, feat, heat, meat, neat, seat, wheat,
-ell	bell, fell, hell, Nell, sell, swell, tell, well, yell,
-est	best, blest, chest, crest, jest, nest, pest, quest, rest, test, vest, west, zest
-ice	dice, ice, lice, mice, nice, price, rice, slice, splice, twice, vice,
-ick	click, brick, flick, hick, kick, lick, Nick, pick, quick, sick, slick, tick, thick,, trick, wick
-ide	bride, glide, hide, pride, ride, side, slide, tide, wide,
-ight	bright, fright, knight, light, might, night, right, sight, tight,

Rime	Examples
-ill	bill, chill, dill, fill, gill, grill, hill, ill, Jill, kill, mill, pill, quill, shrill, sill, spill, still, till, will
-in	bin, chin, fin, gin, grin, in, kin, pin, sin, spin, thin, tin, twin, win, zin (!)
-ine	dine, fine, line, mine, nine, pine, shine, shrine, twine, wine
-ing	bing, bring, cling, ding, fling, king, ping, ring, sing, sting, string, wing, wring, zing
-ink	blink, brink, clink, drink, ink, kink, link, mink, rink, sink, shrink, stink, think, wink,
-ip	chip, clip, dip, drip, flip, grip, hip, lip, nip, rip, sip, slip, snip, strip, tip, trip, whip, zip
-it	bit, fit, flit, grit, hit, kit, knit, lit, pit, quit, sit, slit, snit, spit, split, zit
-ock	block, clock, crock, dock, flock, jock, knock, lock, mock, rock, shock, sock, stock,
-oke	bloke, broke, choke, coke, joke, poke, smoke, stoke, stroke, woke, yoke,
-op	bop, chop, cop, crop, drop, flop, glop, hop, lop, mop, pop, shop, slop, stop, top
-ore	bore, chore, core, gore, lore, more, shore, snore, sore, store, tore, wore, yore
-ot	blot, clot, cot, dot, got, hot, jot, knot, lot, not, pot, rot, shot, slot, spot, tot, trot
-uck	buck, cluck, duck, Huck, luck, muck, pluck, puck, suck, stuck, struck, tuck, truck, yuck
-ug	bug, chug, drug, dug, glug, hug, jug, mug, plug, rug, shrug, slug, smug, snug, thug, tug
-ump	bump, chump, clump, dump, hump, jump, lump, pump, rump, slump, stump, thump
-unk	Bunk, chunk, clunk, drunk, dunk, funk, gunk, hunk, junk, plunk, punk, sunk, stunk

The table on pages 139 and 140 contains examples of single-syllable words containing a rime from Wylie and Durrell's list of the 37 most frequently occurring rimes in early grade reading. These words (and others) are counted if they end in the rime (i. e. no plural or possessive marker and no suffix). Thus, count *duck*, but not *ducks* (plural), *duck's* (possessive), or *ducks, ducked, ducking* (verb forms).

Children find that grouping words by rime gives them confidence and a feeling of control. The rime patterns form the pathways for memorisation. Teachers need to show children that patterns are valuable as well as helping children to develop a habit of continually making analogies. In order to encourage children to do this, teachers can:

- model how to make an analogy by matching new words to a known pattern
- draw attention to the features of new words: *What does 'sit' look like? Do you know another word that looks or sounds like it?*
- discuss patterns: *'Cow'. I know another word like it ... 'now'. Do you know one? I know a longer word, too ... 'brown'. Can you hear the sound 'ow' in the middle?*
- focus on patterns in spelling quizzes: *bake, cake, lake, take*
- encourage the guessing of words based on known rimes
- revise spoken tongue twisters, pointing out the role of onset and rime.

Neurological research now confirms that patterns are passages that a child's memories follow, forming links between existing knowledge and the new input. Recognising patterns in language and also in numbers is the system by which we all form long-term memories. Memorising facts in isolation, not linked to meaningful 'doing', can be confusing for the young child and the facts are less likely to be retained.

Many English spelling patterns are dependent on groups of letters standing for groups of phonemes. Decoding words using the onset and rime method suggests an easier way to look at words and recognise patterns than trying to memorise and use phonic rules.

7.4 Teacher's role

7.4.1 Tutor-talks

Phonics information, although de-emphasised, is introduced in mini tutor-talks where the teacher takes a word from context and talks about it in an interesting, easy-to-memorise way. Tutor-talks occur naturally to fill a need. They are often based on phonics elements that children find difficult or on a new rime pattern found in a story, song or project. Although some of these talks are impromptu, others are planned to fit in with the hidden syllabus. Tutor-talks can be thought of in these categories:

- Spontaneous scaffolding or explanation to give further information
- Planned explanation during discussions about word patterns and analogies
- History of words (origin/meaning/use)
- Preliminary discussions about the role of grammar and punctuation

Tutor-talks about words should be linked to spelling preparation for spelling quizzes. Quizzes should also include a selection of words with the same pattern as another way of consolidating analogies.

For analytic phonics to be taught successfully, teachers need to feel confident that they can explain sufficiently well to support children and parents, too. Teachers also need to feel sufficiently inspired by language in order to take children beyond decoding text to enjoying reading and words.

7.4.2 Supplying further reading books and materials

Reading is learned though reading, and spelling is learned through reading. Once children begin to read, they need to continue reading to become fluent. Reading scheme books or picture books need to be taken home, since a regular five- to ten-minute slot a day with parents not only helps consolidate reading, but motivates children.

Many schools move on to reading schemes which include words for their phonic structure, rather than their beauty or relevance to the language/text, and this can sometimes detract from children's interest in reading. Furthermore, in some cases reading scheme texts are not relevant to children's own life experience, as they portray English-speaking contexts and societies. These schemes therefore need to be supplemented with other books and materials of the right level that can stimulate imagination, helping children develop a love of reading (see Chapter 11, page 226).

Children also want and need to read more than their reading scheme books. However, finding good 'real books' (fiction and/or non-fiction) suitable for emergent readers and their interests is not always easy. As an alternative, teachers and children can create and print class newsletters containing suitable short texts and images from magazines. This makes fun reading for young children.

'Class News': making a newsletter

The class could have two separate newsletters (for example 'Boys' News' and 'Girls' News', or 'Sports news' and 'Animal news') if the children have very different interests.

The teacher selects and cuts cut out a range of suitable material (more than needed), and creates a newsletter template.

The teacher appoints two Editors for each paper.
In the first few editions, the teacher helps children choose what to include from the bank of pre-selected material, modelling how to limit the amount of text.

Children stick their chosen texts on to the newsletter template. The teacher copies the newsletters, distributing them to each child and to other teachers in the school.

Once established, more responsibility can be handed over to the children.

Parents can also be included in the selection of material.

Figure 11 A class newsletter

Tuesday February 9th 2015

Crocodiles can't chew.

NEWS & VIEWS

Humans can make **10,000** different facial expressions.

Fish can't close their **eyes.**

USA
Mr. Eiffel also created the internal frame of the Statue of Liberty in 1886.

MOUNT EVEREST IS ABOUT **27** TIMES TALLER THAN THE EIFFEL TOWER.

Earth's temperature rises slightly during a full **moon.**

In 1865, it was named Mount Everest, after Sir George Everest

Everest is 29,035 feet or 8848 meters high

There are 18 different climbing routes on Everest

It takes 40 days to climb Mt. Everest

MR. EIFFEL

NOT A BAD JOB IF I SAY SO MYSELF.

Alexandre Gustave Eiffel

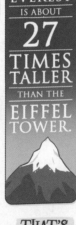

THAT'S
The Eiffel Tower
Paris France

7.4.3 Assessing

Children can become fluent readers practically overnight, much to their surprise. Any assessing by the teacher may not accurately show what stage they have reached. Some assessment can be made by noticing miscues that show where a child needs extra help. Any miscues should not be regarded as mistakes, but rather as learning opportunities. Over-correction can de-motivate children and leave them not wanting to read aloud or with parents.

Reading schemes follow a graded syllabus of phonics. Teachers and parents assess children's reading ability by the 'level' that their graded reading book is at, for example, 'Level 6' or 'Blue band'. Children in many schools have their own reading log book, which records the name of each book read. Many have an additional space for parents' comments. Each child may read to the teacher individually once a week, on average, but more frequently in small groups.

It is a good idea for teachers to keep notes on the following when listening to children read:

- How does the child use context clues?
- Can the child break words into syllables?
- Does the child use syllables to decode long words?
- How does the child tackle new words?
- Does the child go back and correct him/herself or wait for adult help?
- Does the child like a second try?
- Does the child go back to books he/she read some time ago to see how well he/she can read them now?
- Does the child begin to read with expression, no longer reading staccato and over-blending?
- Does the child put character into reading what people say?
- Is it better if you co-read and model the text before the child reads?

7.4.4 Becoming fluent readers

Learning to read develops through reading. However, learning the techniques of reading should not dominate to such an extent that children forget that reading is for communication and enjoyment. During each lesson, or just before the end of the lesson, teachers should find time to read a simple picture book or rhyme to children for enjoyment, sometimes recording it for children to listen to again at home or school. Ideally, children should have their own copies of books and have access to borrowing good fiction and non-fiction picture books. Through reading picture books children are naturally exposed to various genres of English language.

Young children appear to get great satisfaction from reading aloud, especially to teachers. They continually ask when it is their turn and are disappointed if they do not get a chance in every lesson. Reading aloud seems to motivate and to give satisfaction. Children do not seem to mind reading the same text over and over again, and each time they self-correct and refine their performance. Reading aloud to the teacher also gives children an added opportunity to have personal contact with the teacher, and enables the teacher to hear any mistakes and assess the child's decoding techniques. Self-recording on a phone or tablet gives children opportunities to hear their mistakes and self-correct.

Children learn from imitating, and if we want them to read well it is necessary for them to hear a good model of reading. Models can be either the teacher reading or a recording. However, for young children there is no substitute for the teacher and personal contact.

In any class it is easy to identify, by their progress, children who regularly read aloud to parents or participate in shared reading. These opportunities act as tutorial experiences.

Children should never be expected to read aloud any material they have not already encountered orally. The material that is read aloud should not be limited to just the textbook or reader, but should include notices, lists, invitations and other material connected with classroom activities.

If a child is not making progress in reading and is gradually beginning to fall behind the others, it is important to find out the reason as soon as possible and take some action. It may be that the child has not had sufficient opportunities to consolidate. If this is the case, a revision programme based on cards and games is often sufficient to bring a slower reader up to standard. The stimulus of a different reading book or a new project can sometimes also get results.

As children grow in confidence and have more diverse experiences their multi-strategies to decode become more efficient and, like adults, they unconsciously decode a word and read it. If you ask them how they decoded it, they may find difficulty in explaining. The more practice children have in reading, the sooner they become able to read with fluency. Reading is learned by reading experience. Here is one experience:

At the end of each day, ten to fifteen minutes before going home, the children gathered on the floor round the teacher's chair. The teacher went over work done during the day, discussed work for the following day and then read part, or all, of a picture book. The choice of book was made alternately by the teacher and one of the groups in the class. The groups always chose a book the teacher had previously read. However, the teacher always introduced a new story.

We cannot push children to read before they are ready ... when ready it goes quickly.

(Whitehead)

We should spend as much time as possible immersing all children in the sound, feel and meaning of the written language, so that they can hear and feel the way it works.

(Rosen)

8

Introducing handwriting

8.1   The role of handwriting

Handwriting is a lifetime skill, so it is important to start from the beginning with correct hand movement habits that will lead on to writing a 'good hand'. Signatures are still needed in everyday life but handwritten letters for job applications are not usually requested nowadays (even though their handwriting style sometimes reveals more than the actual content). Technology and the modern pace of life have changed this, but nevertheless *How to Improve your Handwriting* books continue to sell well!

With new types of technology becoming more easily available and used by young children long before they have sufficient motor skills to handwrite, some parents ask *Why bother to introduce handwriting now? Why not leave it until much later?*

> *Handwriting is a manual skill and craft with artistic dimensions. It is concerned only with the formation of the written symbols used in a culture and as such it should be legible and pleasing.*
>
> (Sassoon)

The important role of handwriting in holistic development, and especially brain development, should not be disregarded. Neither should the support that handwriting contributes to consolidating early literacy skills. Although handwriting skills cannot be replaced by keyboard-writing activities on screen, these activities, if well chosen, can also complement holistic development and broaden learning.

Postponing learning to handwrite until later when children have finer muscular control and greater hand-eye coordination could be an option, but equally could be a handicap as children show an innate desire to physically use their hands to imitate role models and create. Children want to 'learn by doing'. Also, at this age children's movements are still flexible and more easily trained, as we know from music, ballet and sports teachers and trainers.

In the early years it is important to identify two types of writing:

Handwriting: a skill involving copying the Roman capital and small letters correctly and writing them legibly. Handwriting needs to be a tutored skill for young children if letters are to be formed in the correct way, enabling the handwriting to flow naturally onto cursive (joined-up) writing later on.

Self-created writing: where a text is created in order to communicate information, for example, to tell a story. The text can be handwritten or created using a keyboard, or even written with moveable alphabet letters on a white board or table top.

Interestingly, from the very early stages of handwriting young children develop an individual handwriting style that is recognisable as theirs by others – both adults and children. It is an expression of their own identity. A teacher might say when returning work to the class *This hasn't got a name on it, but I know it is Jim's by the handwriting. Am I right?*

- Handwriting is the physical link between the spoken and self-created written word. It is a taught skill that becomes a creative activity – an unconscious, individual expression of the inner self, and something that children should take pride in. (Text on screen with added smiley-face icons cannot convey the same depth of feeling!)
- Self-created writing for communication is a uniquely personal creative statement. It is a physical expression of the desire to inform, to influence, to celebrate and make other declarations. Writing something is a way of recording thoughts and making them official, permanent and accessible to others.
- Individual handwriting and the way it is designed on a page is an innovative and creative experience open to any young child, if materials are available.

8.2 Beginning handwriting

Handwriting follows on from learning to recognise letters and words, and most children can read written language before handwriting skills have been completely mastered.

However, most children who are ready to read have already acquired the muscular motor skills and hand-eye coordination needed for pencil control. They have also learned in LI about the skills of handwriting and copying, though they may not yet be 'fluent' handwriters. (Fluent writers can write without consciously having to think about, or verbalise, how to form each letter or character. Fluent writers won't be heard saying *letter b … down to the bottom, up, and around*. They also understand that if letters or characters are not accurately and clearly written, they cannot be decoded and can cause confusion!)

Young children who already write Roman script find no particular difficulty in writing English. They should be allowed to write either in a printed (non-cursive) style which matches the font of their first English textbooks, or in the same style as they write in LI. Many teachers have noticed, however, that some children who already write LI in cursive (joined-up) Roman letters choose to write English in print script during the first stages of learning.

Children whose LI script or writing direction is different from English also soon learn to write in English, when presented with a structured programme of letter formation based on stroke order (see 8.8 on). This is because the basic concepts of what writing represents (encoding) have already been learned in LI.

Secret languages and codes seem to fascinate young children and many seem interested in being able to write English, which they see as another type of 'cool' code. To be able to write in English also provides written 'proof' of progress for both children and parents. This visual and permanent sign of progression gives satisfaction that motivates.

If children are to write quickly and legibly when older, they have to learn from the beginning how to form the letters correctly, using the correct stroke order and direction. For example, circle letters (**a c d**) are formed anticlockwise, otherwise the handwriting does not naturally flow. Letters which are written using the wrong 'routes' and stroke orders hamper progress as they do not allow the forwards flow that gives the speed necessary for later cursive (joined-up) writing.

Establishing the correct routes and stroke orders in handwriting takes time and effort. Playful repetition at this early stage, along with continual assessment, is an investment for the future, however, because once bad handwriting habits form they are much more difficult to eradicate.

Example activity to support letter formation routes

Make a big *O* for a face (anticlockwise *O*).

A smaller *o* for each of the eyes, another *o* for the nose and another *o* for the mouth.

Draw a fly on the nose!

Draw the hair sticking up in surprise by straight down strokes to the head (descending small *l*).

Add a neck and a necklace of beads (backward strokes) or a football scarf!

Figure 12 Letter faces

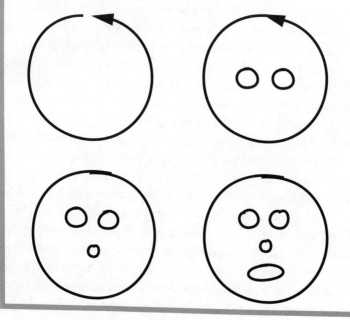

8.2.1 How to introduce handwriting

Handwriting should be introduced with the small letters first, as most text we read consists mainly of small letters. Words written in small letters are easier to recognise than those written in capitals. Capitals are generally used to fill in forms, for emphasis in written text (for example, *STOP!*), or to attract attention on signs and notices. Apart from their own names, or initial capitals for sentence writing, children won't really need to use capitals much in the early stages of writing. If children are taught to write capital letters first, they naturally write their first words all in capitals. Once they have developed this habit it can be difficult to break, and words often get written like this:

DaDDy

Some parents are under the misapprehension that capitals are easier for young children to write and they therefore try to teach them to their children first. Some parents may have learned a different style of letter formation when they went to school and want to show their children a different way from the teacher. It is important for teachers not to comment or criticise as it can demotivate both parents and children. Teachers may find it advisable to explain beforehand to parents (in a class meeting or via a letter home) how they are going to be teaching writing. They could give parents a copy of the Roman script they will be using (small and capital letters) and ask the parents to help their child by using the same style of script.

As soon as children can recognise the small Roman letters, they are ready to begin learning how to write them. Learning to handwrite is rather like an apprenticeship. The adult demonstrates while the child looks. The child then does it alone, while the adult encourages and guides. Demonstrations can include making the movement of the letter shape using an index or middle finger on the palm of the other hand or by writing in sand. This type of tactile demonstration should be done *before* writing on paper with a soft-leaded pencil, so that that children get the 'feel' of the movement made by the letter (for example, a backwards/ anticlockwise circle, or a descending stroke – both of which may be new to children who write in a different script).

Teaching how to form the letters is important. Once children have learned how to make the letters 'the right way' these movements become second nature. It is important to go slowly. More practice in the early stages makes the later stages easier, as there is less need for focused remedial handwriting.

> **Practice makes perfect.**
>
> (old English proverb)

Meaningful opportunities to handwrite something each day, or many times in a week, develop the necessary muscular control and hand-eye coordination. Children can self-focus where to practise and they will self-assess their improvement; any show of improvement is sufficient to self-motivate. It is through practice that the child develops the necessary movement skills. Not until the child has mastered the basic movements to make the letters does he or she begin, unconsciously, to insert his or her own creativity into handwriting.

8.2.2 Developing handwriting skills

Handwriting is a creative activity in which individuality becomes unconsciously embedded. It is one of the few creative activities still used nearly every day. Teachers can encourage this in the classroom by creating opportunities for children to sign their work, fill in the register, or write in little books (see Chapter 7, page 134).

- The point at which writing becomes an unconscious, holistic skill depends on the individual and is not necessarily linked to intellectual abilities. Handwriting skills increase with maturity. For some children, especially boys, it is often better to explain how letters are formed and then praise all efforts, rather than insisting on neat handwriting. This applies until the age of around 8, when finer muscular control has developed.
- Many teachers observe that muscular control and coordination tends to develop later in boys (and some left-handers) than girls. Comparison of boys' achievements with girls' neat work should always be avoided, as it can be

discouraging when boys have tried their best. Girls, not understanding the situation at this age, can sometimes make insensitive remarks about tidiness, which can hurt feelings (see Chapter 5, page 83).

- Check the way the pencil is held in L1 as it may be different from the way it should be held when writing Roman letters (this is usually the case for Japanese and Chinese characters). Check whether each child is right- or left-handed (see 8.2.3).

- Co-sharing written activities (teacher–child or child–child), and using individual alphabet letters to write words and play word games, can help to satisfy an impulse to write (create) in English.

- Some children need more practice than others to achieve. If paper and pencils are always available, girls often initiate their own practice sessions, sitting down together in free-play times or doing extra writing for homework. Boys find initiating self-practice more difficult.

- Include activities where children copy known text (i.e. text that that they can read). This allows them to focus purely on handwriting skills without the burden of decoding the content (see 8.2.4).

- Handwriting skills are creative and holistic. They reflect the 'feel-good factor'. If a child is unwell or emotionally upset and has an 'off day', it is often reflected in their handwriting.

- Finger rhymes and focused handwork activities also help to develop muscular movement and eye-hand coordination. Colouring in can also increase control, but colouring in large areas within an outline created by an adult may have little meaning for children.

8.2.3 Which hand? Right or left?

Worldwide attitudes to left-handedness have changed considerably, with increasing levels of understanding. There is more information and support available on the Internet these days and left-handed materials (for example, pens and scissors) are also now available for children, simplifying the acquisition of fine motor skills.

It is said to be easier to write Roman letters with the right hand, and also more difficult to write characters used in Chinese and Japanese script with the left. However, most young children are flexible and take on the challenge of learning a different script in their stride.

Naturally left-handed children need support, however, if they are not to feel too different or isolated. One way to raise awareness is to play a game about famous people who were or are left-handed. Children discuss a pre-prepared list of such people and then search for others in their own country or local society. The children could play an 'I spy' game, looking for and counting how many adults or children they notice writing with their left hand within a single day.

Famous left-handed people

Alexander the Great, Julius Caesar, Leonardo Da Vinci, Napoleon Bonaparte, Charlie Chaplin, Albert Einstein, Winston Churchill, Mahatma Ghandi, Neil Armstrong, Bill Gates, Robert de Niro, Tom Cruise, Prince William, Rafael Nadal

Also, at least five US Presidents, including Barack Obama, Bill Clinton, George W. Bush (Senior), Ronald Reagan and Gerald Ford

---

Figure 13 Handwriting positions for right- and left-handers

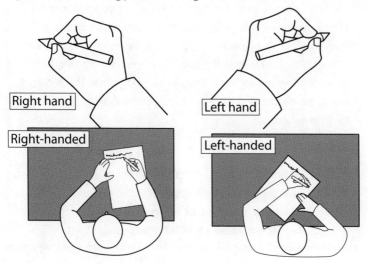

Right hand

Right-handed

Left hand

Left-handed

Right handers

Children who write with the right hand should place their paper slightly to the right-hand side of their body to facilitate movement from left to right. The paper should be placed parallel to the bottom of the desk, but as movement takes place it can become slightly tilted to the left. The pencil should be held lightly between the thumb and first finger, about 1 inch (2.5 centimetres) from the tip, with the middle finger providing additional support. The other two fingers can rest lightly on the paper. The pencil should be placed on the paper in a position between about ten and eleven on a clock, that is about 45° to the left of the upright.

Left handers

Children who write with the left hand should hold the pencil in the same way as right-handed children, except that the grip should be further away from the point to enable children to see what they have written, and the unsharpened end should point towards the body. This position helps to avoid the natural inclination of the left-hander to push the hand to write. The paper should be placed on the left side of the body at a steep slope towards the body in order to enable the hand to pull away from the writing. Other styles (for example, the 'claw' style where the arm is placed above the line and the hand is hooked round to hold the pencil) are to be discouraged as they make speed handwriting difficult to achieve later.

Check:

- Are children holding their pencils correctly?
- Are they sitting with their paper placed in the correct position? (This is especially important for left-handers.)
- Does their writing follow a neat line (real or imaginary)?

8.2.4 Handwriting practice

Copying known text is an important, often misunderstood, step in learning to write. It enables the child to focus exclusively on improving handwriting skills, without the burden of having to decode or create text. Copying also helps to reinforce memorisation of how words are spelt (see Chapter 9, page 191).

Children often enjoy trying again and again to achieve a good piece of work. Teachers should ensure children are writing with the correct utensil (a soft pencil) and should allow children to rub out and self-correct letter shapes where they feel they can do better. Praise should be given for tenacity and effort!

Copying known text:

* is a basic step in holistic literacy development, providing focus on handwriting whilst giving broader experience in written language and spelling
* is useful reinforcement as children often recite the text to themselves word by word as they write
* enables a child to focus fully on his or her handwriting skills, since it involves only one task (copying)
* is useful for providing 'show-off' pieces of work that record progress in both handwriting and reading the known text
* can be followed by children adding their own creative design, pattern or picture to complete the experience.

8.3 Initial assessment

To teach handwriting effectively, it is important to assess each child. Teachers can make a quick, initial assessment to find out about each child's level of hand control, type of hand control (position of fingers and thumb) and method of making Roman letters.

The teacher can ask the child to write the numbers 0 to 5 or 10 (depending on the developmental age). Whilst the child writes, the teacher observes the movements used to make each number (although the actual shape of the number is not relevant since number shapes vary in different societies). The results can be compared with the number formation guidelines given below. If children are not yet writing digits using the correct stoke order and direction, teachers should work to correct this before moving on to letters.

---

0   anticlockwise or clockwise movement?

I   starting at the top and descending, or starting at bottom and going up?

2   starting at top and descending (going clockwise)?

3   one stroke starting at the top and going demi-clockwise twice?

4   two strokes starting at top?

5   two strokes from the top left of the digit, with the straight line across the top (left to right) being added *after* the main stroke?

6   anticlockwise movement, starting from the top?

7   one stroke or two, and starting from the top or from the bottom?

8   a letter 'S' starting from top or two letter 'o's one on top of the other?

9   clockwise movement?

8.4 Stimulating children to handwrite

Sometimes it is necessary to encourage a child's desire to write, especially for boys who don't like to sit still for too long. Teachers should remember that once interest in a writing activity begins to wane, it is time to move on to something else. The activity can be completed in the next lesson or, if reasonable, finished off at home.

Extending an activity to the point of loss of interest can be counterproductive and put children off writing. Below are some simple ideas for stimulating an interest in handwriting:

Writing letters to classmates

The teacher makes a postbox for the classroom from cardboard boxes, with a slit for posting letters.

Children handwrite a simple message or greeting to a classmate on illustrated or coloured paper. The paper is folded and the classmate's name is written on the outside. The 'letter' is then 'posted' in the classroom postbox.

Before home time, a class 'post person' opens the postbox and delivers the letters. The teacher can add his or her own letters (with more advanced text) to ensure that all children receive a letter each week.

Copying known rhymes onto cards

Children choose a known rhyme to copy onto card, decorate with pictures and then display in the classroom (see Chapter 6, page 101 for examples of rhymes).

8.4.1 Exhibiting work

Children learn much from each other's work. In fact, often more is learned from other children's ideas of presentation, design and layout than from explanations given by the teacher or parent. Work done at home or during the lesson should be displayed in the classroom. If possible, it is a good idea to keep children's work over a period of a term or a year in a folder, so that they and their parents can track the development in their writing skills.

8.4.2 Tutor-talks

Handwriting has to be taught carefully, following a graded programme (see 8.8), with many opportunities to imitate the teacher's writing model. This is particularly true for children who are non-writers or who have a non-Roman-script L1.

Tutor-talks specifically about punctuation are best left until children are writing more fluently, and with real communicative purpose. However, when punctuation naturally occurs, explanations should be given. When children copy text, they will probably copy punctuation marks and this will create opportunities to talk naturally about common punctuation marks and when to use them.

8.5 Style

The style of handwriting to be taught is likely to be decided by the school handwriting policy or the course textbook. Where choice is available, however, teachers have to decide whether to use:

- a print style matching (or close to) the text used in textbooks
- a print style which includes a 'flick' at the bottom of each letter, to prepare children to move on easily to joined-up writing.

It is important that parents use the same handwriting style the teacher is using at school when helping their children to write at home. Some parents may still use 'ball and stick' letters that are made with too many strokes, as that was the way they were taught as beginners in school. Ball and stick movements do not lead onto cursive writing so children have to learn different movements for speed handwriting.

It is thought that teaching native-English-speaking children pre-cursive handwriting with a 'flick' from the very beginning takes longer. However, in the end it saves time as it leads on naturally to cursive

Figure 14 Ball and stick handwriting method (not encouraged)

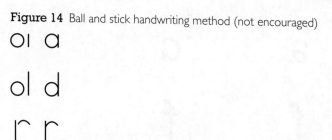

handwriting, meaning children only have to learn one way to handwrite letters.

Despite this, children with a non-Roman-script L1 may find that writing simple print versions of letters (without flicks) is easier to begin with. This is because simple, written print matches more closely the print they are learning to read (decode) and beginning to spell (encode). Once the children's ability to recognise and match print and handwritten letters is more developed, the transfer over to cursive handwriting is quick since muscular control and hand-eye coordination has already been built up via learning to write simple print (as well as the L1 script).

Teaching a non-simplified cursive handwriting (such as the D'Nealian style often taught in the United States) from the first step can be confusing unless teachers can write it well themselves, quickly and without faults. Some children are already aware of different font styles from playing on the computer and seeing them on screen. Once they can handwrite well, it can be interesting to introduce them to different fonts and challenge them in games to decode them.

Tutor-talk helps children to understand and recognise that some small letters can have a printed style that varies slightly from the handwritten style (for example, they may have a different shape, or a different position on the baseline of the text). These letters are:

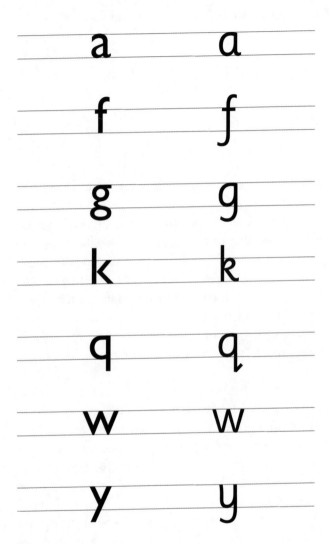

Handwriting can be self-taught as children already understand the concept of encoding language. However, it is better if it is taught through tutor-talk as children can then learn how to make letters 'the right way' for later cursive writing. Going slowly at the beginning, revising and confirming how to make the strokes correctly, is economical in the long term.

Although first writing is in print or pre-cursive style, decoding and copying text from picturebooks is becoming more difficult for L2 learners because in some books text is no longer presented in one style throughout. Many picturebook publishers now prefer to concentrate on the overall design of the page, mixing font styles (as well as capital and small letters) with illustrations to reflect emotions and create a feeling of novelty and surprise. This makes decoding complicated and possibly even discouraging for the early L2 reader, unless an adult co-shares the reading and guides the child through the decoding 'maze'.

8.6 Materials

The quality of paper is important as children are initially going to rub out (erase) letters in order to self-correct. Paper shouldn't be so thin that it will tear or disintegrate when children erase mistakes. This is demotivating for children and might put them off writing. Notebooks with narrowly spaced lines or small squares are not suitable for children as they don't yet have the necessary fine motor skills to be able to write within narrow lines. Ideally children need special paper with lines to guide them on positioning and sizing of letters (see 8.8).

Handwriting must flow easily and to obtain an easy flow it is essential that the writer has a light touch. For a Chinese child, for example, the change from writing counted strokes within a square (Chinese Characters) to writing cursively entails a change in hand pressure as well as in hand movements. In countries where the handwriting system is different from Roman script, it is better to encourage children to use a special pencil

Figure 15 Chinese Characters

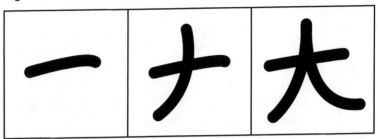

just for writing in English. This helps children to make the transfer to the different handwriting system.

Children need to use a pencil or writing utensil that requires the use of very little pressure. For this reason, they should be introduced to writing with a very soft pencil (2B) with a blunt point. Electric pencil sharpeners give too fine a point to obtain a smooth flow when writing Roman letters (although they are ideal for writing Chinese characters!). As young children gain in skill they can move on to using a harder B pencil and eventually HB. It should be remembered that most ballpoint pens and other disposable pens require a lot of pressure to get an even flow and are thus not advisable for writing in the early habit-forming stage.

Teachers need to make sure pencils are easy to hold and not too short. The child should hold the pencil far enough away from the point to see what is being written. If held too close to the tip, the child will not be able to see what he or she has written immediately.

8.7 Handwriting size

Young children cannot write very small letters as they do not yet have fine enough muscular control. Writing very large letters is also difficult for young children, as this also requires well-developed muscular control. For young children who already write L1 in another script, the mid line (the 'x' height) of the handwriting should be approximately 5 mm in size.

Gradually, as children grow in competence, the size can be reduced to 4 mm. The space between lines needs to be wide enough for descending letters not to mix with ascending letters on the next line.

Children with a non-Roman-script L1 can benefit from learning to write with 'tracks'. Consisting of three or four guidelines, tracks can help children get used to the relative size and proportions of capital and small letters. The tracks guide children on the general size of letters, as well as on how high or low to go above or below the line when writing ascending and descending letters. It is helpful to provide paper with tracks for a short period.

Figure 16 Writing on tracks

1. Three guide line tracks

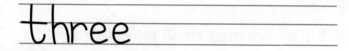

2. Four guide line tracks

Once young children have sufficient experience, the number of guide lines can be reduced to two and then just one (the 'base line'). As children become fluent handwriters they will use only the base line to develop their own size of writing.

Young children seem to have none of the fears and apprehensions of older children about their skill in writing on unlined paper. After two or three efforts they manage surprisingly well, writing in reasonably straight lines on plain paper and developing a natural feel for presentation and layout. Many young children appear to have an ability to estimate size and it is important in handwriting that opportunities are given for them to develop these natural skills of estimation and presentation. This is another aspect of developing innovation and creativity.

8.8   Handwriting programme

Letters should be made in the simplest way using as few strokes as possible and concentrating on natural movements of the hand, movements which children have made since they first started scribbling on paper. These natural movements lead on quickly and easily to cursive (joined-up) writing.

8.8.1 Introducing small letters

Teachers need to check children are using the correct pencil hold. Some children manage to achieve a surprisingly high standard of writing holding their pencil in unorthodox ways. However, if the utensil for writing Roman script is not held correctly, writing at speed, which becomes a necessary skill at a later stage, is difficult. If the correct habits of stroke order and hold are developed from the first lessons, later cursive writing develops naturally and quickly (see 8.5). As in most skills, faults acquired in the early stages of handwriting are difficult and time-consuming to eradicate.

Children want to use their knowledge of how to write letters to form words as soon as possible. After completing the first six steps of the structured programme on page 169, they can write some simple, known words.

go   stop   dog

After completing all nine steps of the programme, young children can write in small letters and should be encouraged to do so. However, the capital letters should be introduced as quickly after this as possible, following a graded programme.

Figure 17 Structured programme for introducing small letters in simple print style

To make each letter, the writer puts his or her pencil point on the circular dot and continues the stroke following the arrow head – there are 33 strokes in all.

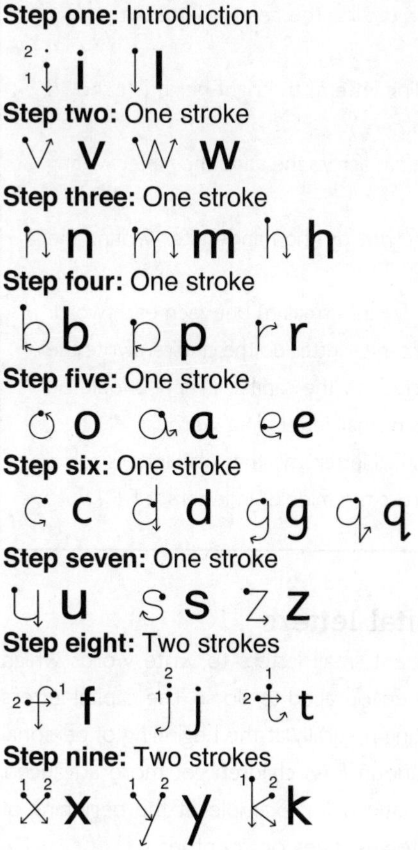

Step one: Introduction

i i l l

Step two: One stroke

v v w w

Step three: One stroke

n n m m h h

Step four: One stroke

b b p p r r

Step five: One stroke

o o a a e e

Step six: One stroke

c c d d g g q q

Step seven: One stroke

u u s s z z

Step eight: Two strokes

f f j j t t

Step nine: Two strokes

x x y y k k

Small alphabet letters with flicks can be introduced in the same stroke order. A chart in the Appendix (page 237) shows how to write the 26 letters. It is thought that the added flick makes moving on to joined-up (cursive) writing easier and faster.

169

Teachers should check and discuss the following points with the children:

- Are the letters sitting on the base line?
- Are the letters that go below the line (descending letters) the right length?
- Are the tall letters (ascending letters) the right height? (*t* should not be quite as tall as the others.)
- Are the children putting the bar across the *t* and the *f* after writing the down stroke?
- Are the children putting the dot on the *i* and *j* after writing the down stroke?
- Is there a space (the same size as a small *o*) between each word?
- When a word begins with a capital letter, do the children write the small letters which follow close to the capital? (There should be no more space than between small letters in a word.)
- When mixing capitals and small letters, do the small letters come as high as the 'gate' (line across the middle) in letters *A F E H?*

8.8.2 Introducing capital letters

As soon as children know sufficient small letters to write words which they know orally, they should be encouraged to do so. The capital letters can then be introduced into writing naturally at the beginning of personal names and for the personal pronoun *I*. As children get more advanced, capitals can be used in other situations, for example, at the beginning of sentences or for the names of towns, cities or countries.

The use of capitals may be difficult for children who are not used to two sizes and forms for each letter. Arabic, Japanese and Chinese writing systems do not have any comparable form, for example. Furthermore, in some European languages capitals are used differently from in English.

Figure 18 Structured programme for introducing capital letters

Step one

Step two

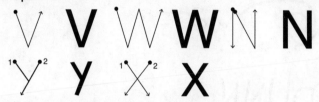

Step three

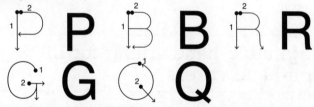

Step four

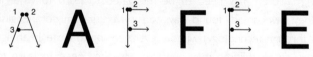

Children always enjoy making up ways to sign their name. Signatures become great points for discussion and are frequently altered throughout childhood. Teachers can ask children to write their signature and then underneath to print out their name using capital letters. This can develop into an interesting project, with teachers extending the task to include the collection of signatures from the whole class as well as family members (with all names printed out in capital letters too).

Figure 19 A child's signature

N.J.DUNN

(7 years 1 month)

8.9   Beginning handwriting for L1 non-handwriters

8.9.1 Motivation and purpose for writing

Some young children may need to be motivated to learn to write in English as they have already found ways to survive using only oral English (spoken, or through technology) without ever needing to write. In an age of technology, some children may question why they need to learn to handwrite in English at all, or for that matter in L1!

To provide examples for children of purposeful handwriting, the teacher could write notes to parents in English, for example.

For some children, finding out about how to encode English (handwriting or texting) comes naturally if their environment has been rich in purposeful experiences, They may, for example, have seen adult role models writing lists, notes and emails. Children may also have been influenced by older children or the media, and therefore think it is 'cool' to write English.

Figure 20 A note to parents

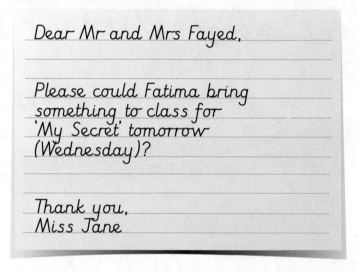

Dear Mr and Mrs Fayed,

Please could Fatima bring something to class for 'My Secret' tomorrow (Wednesday)?

Thank you,
Miss Jane

8.9.2 Writing patterns

Illustrations and patterns which accompany copying or writing at this stage are very important for young learners who are not yet writing in L1. Patterns are equivalent to the drawings very young children make to express their ideas pictorially, before they have sufficient language to express them in the same verbal detail.

Writing patterns helps to develop finer muscular control and the movements necessary for cursive writing. It also introduces children to a self-creative design activity (other than drawing) which can be important for children who find difficulty in illustrating.

Figure 21 A writing pattern

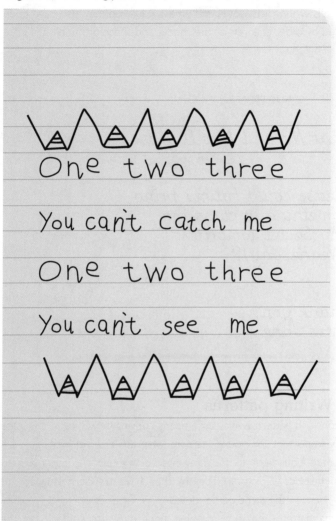

Figure 22 Writing patterns for young non-readers

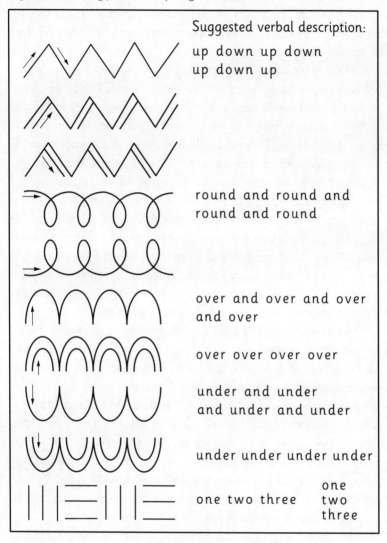

Suggested verbal description:

up down up down
up down up

round and round and
round and round

over and over and over
and over

over over over over

under and under
and under and under

under under under under

one two three   one
                  two
                  three

Writing patterns also helps children to develop the correct movement from left to right, and to gain rhythm and flow. Children appear to enjoy making writing patterns, initially copying them but later enhancing them or building their own designs.

Children who can already write in LI are generally keen to get on with writing the letters in English. For these children, it is better to skip an initial pattern writing stage as it may dampen some of their enthusiasm. In these cases, it is better to teach the letters and any related patterns at the same time. At a later stage children can be given opportunities to use writing patterns to decorate pieces of writing, cards, invitations, etc.

Once children who cannot write in LI are familiar with the basic writing patterns, they can be introduced to the alphabet following the groupings of the structured writing programmes (see 8.8.1 and 8.8.2 on pages 169 and 171). It is important that young children can see a demonstration of how to make each letter clearly. Children find it helpful if the teacher talks about what she is doing whilst making a pattern or letter. For example, the teacher could say *Go down and up* whilst making a zig-zag pattern, or *Go down and then make a dot* whilst writing the letter *i*.

Children often want to repeat what the teacher has said whilst making the pattern or the letter themselves. They frequently continue describing what they are doing aloud until they have internalised the process. For very young children visual and kinesthetic cues, as well as verbal descriptions, seem necessary for successful learning. Therefore, children should also be given the opportunity to feel the shape of letter, perhaps by handling plastic shaped letters or by outlining the letters on their hands.

It is best for very young children to make patterns and letters on plain paper. The initial size of patterns and letters will be determined by each individual child's muscular development and degree of practice, and by the type of writing implement used (see 8.6).

Although many children now write on computers, there is holistical neurological importance in forming letters and satisfaction from placing them together to make meaning in words. The fundamental creative expression of making patterns should not be overlooked.

9

Learning to spell

9.1 Spelling (encoding)

Spelling should be a fun activity based on sounds, sound families and syllables in known words, and getting to know their origins! English has absorbed words from different languages and continues to do so, resulting in inconsistent spelling patterns. For example, the letters *ee* in *tree* sound like the letters *ea* in *pea* and *y* in *sunny* and *funny*.

Spelling is interlinked with reading, handwriting and creative writing, and each supports the other. Young children who can already read and write in L1, and thus understand how to spell (encode), are often eager to acquire and use the same skills in English immediately. They want to copy handwriting and also write creatively to communicate in English. The teacher's role is to help them achieve that goal quickly and easily, so that they do not become frustrated.

Children initially need opportunities to find out how to transfer their self-learning strategies from L1 and adjust them to fit the new content in English (see Chapter 2, page 39). Teachers also need to help children progress from focusing on the meaning of words in English to finding out more about how words are spelt (encoded). English words have so many non-phonetic ways of being written, and this can fascinate young children if presented using the Playful Approach (see Chapter 1, page 19). For example, children will enjoy learning about silent letters like *k* (*know, knock, knee*) and *w* (*wrist, write, wreck*).

Young children who pick up English orally unconsciously learn how to use grammar. They manage to apply rules logically without any real awareness of exceptions. Many young children are not yet ready to be taught grammar via formal language analysis, but they are nevertheless interested in finding out more about the language when they learn to encode it.

If children are to become competent and confident spellers, they need to build on their L1 strategies from their 'zone of proximal development' ('ZPD' – see Chapter 2, page 41) in order to develop a broader range of strategies. This can be done via guided tutor-talks.

Being familiar with the sound–letter relationships in English is only one part of spelling. Children also need to be aware that, for example, an added prefix can alter the meaning of a word: *any-thing, no-where*. Elements like this should form part of the teacher's 'hidden syllabus'. Unless children understand how to encode additions to words that alter meanings (for example, prefixes and suffixes), they may not encode correctly. Introducing grammatical or letter changes in a playful way can encourage children to become 'word detectives'. They enjoy playing games which introduce different encodings and meanings (for example, *write/right* and *son/sun*).

Below is a suggested first hidden syllabus. The items are interlinked with reading (decoding), spelling (encoding) and writing for communication. Each point should be introduced and explained in oral examples already known to the children. At this stage, exceptions and additional examples can be included in spoken and written language, when they occur naturally.

Suggested first 'hidden syllabus'

- prefix before a word can alter meaning: *un-do, no-thing, super-star*
- suffix after a word can alter meaning: *in-side, every-where, no-where*
- changing letters at the end of a word can indicate grammatical change
  (e.g. plurals): /s/ sound: a packet, some packets
  - /z/ sound: a hand, two hands
  - /iz/ sound: a face, two faces
- add *n't* to express negation: *isn't, don't, can't*
- add ' to make contractions: *I am / I'm, she is / she's, he is / he's*
- add *'s* to express possession: *Bob's coat, the dog's food*
- add *s* to verbs in third person singular
- subject pronouns: *I/you/we/they/he/she/it*
- add *ly* to make adverbs

Children learning to spell need to appreciate from early on that the sound of a word is only one guide to its spelling.

(O'Sullivan in Dombey and Moustafa)

9.2 Introducing spelling

Teaching children the concept that words which share common sounds often share spellings is a powerful tool to help them on their way to literacy.

(Smith)

To introduce spelling effectively teachers need to know how young children learn (and are still learning) to spell in L1. L1 learning might involve rote learning of imposed rules and words, for example, without recognising and linking patterns. For children changing writing script, skills in handwriting the Roman alphabet should be introduced before focusing on spelling in English. Teachers also need to:

- plan activities (following a hidden syllabus) that enable children to reuse and adjust their L1 strategies to learn English spelling
- present the planned activities using the Playful Approach (see Chapter 1, page 19)
- act as a role model by spelling words aloud and using letter names
- give focused tutor-talks explaining the 'how and why' of spelling.

Spelling in English is complex so providing lower-primary children with lists of traditional spelling rules is ineffectual. It can also be confusing and even off-putting, as many children may not yet be capable of this form of language analysis. Instead, children should take part in interesting activities in which they can listen to and identify language patterns in a meaningful text, supported by focused tutor-talks. This will allow an easy transition to spelling in English.

Rimes are much more reliable in their sound–spelling relationship than are their individual phonemes (basic sound units of speech).

(Dombey)

Listening and visual experiences should come before spelling (encoding). Without a solid foundation of spoken English absorbed through playful, shared language activities (like tongue twisters, rhymes and shared stories), young children may not realise that learning to spell is about recognising patterns in words. They may not be aware that spelling is something they can self-discover, self-learn and also self-control, as there is one standardised model of spelling which they have to match. As in mathematics, there is one right answer.

> *Good spellers like good readers orchestrate a variety of strategies.*
>
> (O'Sullivan in Dombey and Moustafa)

Once the oral foundation is established, children need to be shown how to develop strategies for encoding English through regular tutor-talk explanations, embedded within activities. The explanations should look at and talk about words, and patterns within words, scaffolding what children already know – their 'ZPD' (see Chapter 2, page 41). Each young child's self-learning strategies develop differently and, through regular assessment, teachers can plan how best to support each child and especially those who may have difficulties in learning to spell. When spelling tasks do not relate to children's ZDP (i.e. do not build on patterns they already recognise), children can begin to feel they are bad spellers, losing confidence and become demotivated.

Patterns empower the learning of spelling and are said to be the cement of memory. Every child should have ongoing opportunities to play orally with, for example, made-up or nonsense words, or with lists of rhyming (riming) words with different onsets (*all, b/all, c/all, f/all, h/all, sm/all, t/all* etc. – see Chapter 7, page 139). Teaching children words that share common sounds, and share similar patterns, is a powerful tool to help them become good spellers.

9.2.1 Tutor-talks introducing a 'hidden syllabus'

> *Because of the complicated history of English spelling, few simple rules ever work. There are always exceptions.*
>
> (Crystal)

For children to become competent spellers, teacher tutorials (tutor-talks) are an essential element. English spelling is standardised and there is one correct way to spell. In the initial stages this can be absorbed and understood best through experience with the sounds of words, rather than by relying on rules or memory props like these:

- Rule: *i before e except after c*
- Mnemonic: **b**ig **e**lephants **c**an **a**lways **u**nderstand **s**mall **e**lephants *(because)*
- Saying: *necessary has one collar(c) and two sleeves (ss)*

Spelling tutor-talks should explain:

- how words are spelt aloud using alphabet letter names
- how words are composed of sounds
- how words look, i.e. their shape above and below the line
- what words in phrases or short sentences mean, including explanation of simple grammar items like adjectives and adverbs
- how words are constructed, for example, 'onset and rime' and other word patterns
- how a morpheme unit within words (prefix and suffix) can indicate the function, meaning or pronunciation
- how to make analogies to discover new words, i.e. decoding by linking new words to known words
- that there is a global standard model of how words are encoded (spelt) in English
- that some patterns look and sound alike (*book, cook, look, took* – a short sound) whilst others may look the same but sound different (*spoon, room* – a long sound)
- that in some cases the same sound be can be written in two or more ways (/ee/ *bee, pea, tea, meet, meat, feet, week, cheese*).

Rules and memory props may be useful later, but not in the early stages as they often have exceptions. In addition, they require children to include an additional step in order to memorise a spelling. Instead, the teacher should introduce a series of focused, quick tutor-talks.

> *Helping children to hear and see language patterns in meaningful texts and consistently drawing attention to them in writing, can play a major role in supporting children's spelling development.*

(Dombey)

9.2.2 Self-learning strategies

Once children have broadened their strategies and feel confident enough to draw on them to spell a word, they are on the path to becoming competent spellers who can:

- self-monitor
- self-correct (persevering until their own spelling matches the model)
- self-reflect (developing their individual strategies and 'learning to learn')
- self-analyse (thinking critically and making analogies to understand how a word is constructed).

Poor spellers often have poor phonological awareness and do not naturally use analogy. They have difficulty in making the link between words they hear and words they write and need more individual face-to-face explanations. For example, the teacher may need to ask the child questions such as *What does it look like? What does it sound like?*

Through experience (especially reading aloud) some children appear to develop an innate instinct for how words look; they get a 'feel' for whether the spelling looks right or not. Adults quite often write a word in two different ways to confirm which looks to be the correct spelling. Some children start to use this strategy themselves as they develop their innate 'feel' for how words are spelt. Visual recognition may be stimulated further by 'writing' the shapes of words on the palm of the other hand using the two sensitive fingers (the index and middle finger). It is thought the more you write the more you remember, as memory is learned through the hand.

> *The world can only be grasped by action and contemplation.*
> *The hand is the cutting edge of man.*
>
> (Bronowski)

Self-directed learners can find out a lot about English spelling from collecting English words and phrases used within their society and on screen (for example, from captions, cartoons, adverts, labels and storybooks). Although children may appear to learn more from such sources than from class textbooks, for deep learning to take place they still need the added reinforcement and encouragement that tutor-talks provide.

9.3 Assessing spelling

Many schools have weekly spelling tests, with parents becoming involved in homework preparation for the tests. Tests can represent different emotions in different cultures and may sometimes alter the friendly teacher–child relationship. As children are used to seeing fun quiz programmes on screens, it may be better to change the title of the weekly assessment to 'spelling quiz' and to conduct it with a fun approach. It has to be remembered that the purpose of the quiz is not to find out what the child does not know, but what he or she does know.

If they prepare well, children seem to enjoy spelling quizzes as they have the power to control their result; their answer is either right or wrong. Many children seem to get satisfaction from self-dictating the words to themselves and self-assessing (proofreading) to check whether if they have written all the spellings correctly. Children appear to get great satisfaction in achieving full marks in a spelling quiz. A similar feeling of satisfaction comes from completing a page of easy mathematical sums successfully. *Easy-peasy* children say, having got their spellings right!

9.3.1 The spelling quiz

Regular spelling quizzes can be enjoyable if the approach is playful and the degree of difficulty is structured. Children enjoy listening to the 'music' and rhythm of words spelt out loud. Generally, however, children find it easier if words are broken into syllables (segments): *car/pet, arm/chair, pock/et, com/pu/ter.*

Parents are generally involved as some preparation takes place at home. However, parents need to understand that spelling may be taught differently now from the way they were taught. A spelling quiz should be a fun experience, giving young children opportunities to self-learn. Parents can support children by acting as 'Quiz Master' at home, dictating and checking spelling.

Spelling quizzes provide good opportunities for focused explanations through tutor-talks, as well as showing children their progression. They provide children with opportunities to search for patterns and to organise those patterns into meaningful categories. Patterns help children to see order and build their learning strategies. Chaos can occur when children have not recognised patterns.

Quizzes need to be playfully presented and carefully graded. It is important to start with easy quizzes so that children know they can get all or most of the items right. Having self-confidence is very important.

Young children need to repeat and repeat what appears to adults a pointless activity. It is important not to rush children and not to introduce them to too many of the complexities of English spelling until they have a solid basis, as well as a range of self-learning strategies with which to proceed with confidence.

9.3.2 Selecting quiz content

Quiz content can include words, phrases or short sentences. Some suggested items are given on page 186.

Spelling quiz words with CVC (Consonant-Vowel-Consonant) and CVCC (Consonant-Vowel-Consonant-Consonant):

bag map nap cat man bang

jet net leg red tell

bin lid sit will ring

dog box pop rod dot

bus hut cup pup duck fuss

Useful phrases to include in spelling quizzes (which can be transferred to spoken English):

good and bad	*sad and glad*
in and out	*come and go*
huff and puff	*have got*
inside out	*upside down*
thick and thin	*going there*
slow and sure	*coming here*
please help	*thanks a lot*

Quizzes should be easy to start, with content becoming more complex as self-learning strategies develop. Quizzes should focus on or include:

- patterns
- one or two 'puzzle words' (see Chapter 7, page 123)
- tutor-talk about the words, including examples of the words in known contexts
- simple words relevant to current interests or activities.

Although tutor-talk will refer to the 'onset and rime' (see 9.5) when discussing words to spell, the line between onset and rime should only be made with a finger – not drawn – as the line only exists as a learning prop.

9.3.3 Spelling quiz management

✓ Hold a quiz regularly once a week at a set time. Give several days preparation time.

✓ Make a spelling book for each child, sticking in each week's printed list of words for reference.

✓ Model the word, phrase or short sentence, pronouncing clearly so children can hear the sounds.

✓ Allow children to self-correct, if possible, allowing them to keep secret from others how many they got right!

✓ Follow the same routine each time, leading up to sharing the 'teacher's role' with a child who dictates the spelling words.

✓ Where necessary, divide into groups to match learning abilities, taking care not to cause 'loss of face'. There can be surprises as some children can spell more easily than they can speak. Others can change their ability once they understand how to focus.

9.4 Introducing syllables

Some children find the most effective way to learn to spell longer words is to break them down into discernible parts – syllables or segments. Being able to do this is often undervalued and it is thought to positively influence a child's success in reading.

A syllable is a unit of language consisting of an uninterrupted portion of sound. All words have at least one syllable and each syllable contains at least one vowel sound, with or without surrounding consonants. A multisyllabic word can be divided between two consonants that appear between two vowels (for example, *hap/py, real/ly*). Exceptions to this are consonant digraphs (for example, *ch, th, wh, sh, ph*). These pairings cannot be separated.

Syllables are important in developing phonological awareness as they help children move on from being aware of the meanings of words to being interested in the sequences of sounds that make them. Breaking longer words into smaller units helps children to examine and analyse more than the sound content of words. It alerts them to look for prefixes and suffixes which change meaning.

Syllable song

[Sing to the tune of 'Frère Jacques']

Co/ffee Co/ffee	(2 syllables, *coffee*)
Co/ffee Co/ffee	
Le/mon/ade	(3 syllables, *lemonade*)
Le/mon/ade	
Co/ca Co/ca Co/la	(2 syllables, *Coca* and *Cola*)
Co/ca Co/ca Co/la	
Co/ffee Tea	(1 syllable, *tea*)
Co/ffee Tea	

To help children recognise syllables, either clap rhythmically to each syllable or place one hand firmly under your chin: when you say the word, the chin comes down once on each syllable. Children find it easier to start with two- or three-syllable words, such as *ti/ger, in/to, car/pet, mar/ket, sis/ter, pa/per, chim/pan/zee, e/le/phant*. Useful words to practise syllables with include:

One syllable: *big, small, wrong, right, day, night, high, low, foot, toe*
Two syllables: *lucky, funny, seven, thirteen, twenty, plenty, today*
Three syllables: *unlucky, eleven, seventeen, yesterday, tomorrow*

9.5 Recognising patterns of 'onset and rime'

Patterns of onsets and rimes make up a substantial part of patterning of English spelling.

(Dombey)

Patterns form the passages for memories to follow, linking new learning to existing knowledge by making analogies. Patterns are the system by which long-term memory is formed. Patterns are observations organised into meaningful categories.

In the initial stages of spelling in English, it is easier for young children to recognise patterns if words are divided simply into two clear sections: 'onset and rime'. Children have already initiated play with words with different onset and rime (for example, *c/at, m/at, s/at, h/at, f/at*) when learning to read (see Chapter 7, page 137). This easy-to-understand method introduces an initial analysis of word patterns, which can lead on to more sophisticated encoding (synthetic phonics) as children become more mature and experienced users of English.

Onset

Onset consists of all the letters and phonemes (blends, diagraphs) *before* the first vowel: **b**/oat, **tr**/ain, **pl**/ay.

Rime

Rime continues from the first vowel to the *end* of the word. Through rime the patterns in words are clearly identified. Children can hear and see them more easily: t/*able*, st/*able*, p/*air*, st/*air*, b/*oat*, g/*oat*.

Children enjoy highlighting similar patterns in the same colour. This activity is more than simply colouring as it focuses learning strategies and increasing observation.

9.6 Developing analogy strategies

Children use onset and rime to make analogies between known and unknown words.

(Goswami and Bryant)

Child self-teach in a similar way as when acquiring L1, if given the right enabling opportunities introduced through the Playful Approach. They reuse a strategy to make an analogy between known and new words, interpreting new examples by reference to known patterns. For example, a child who recognises *ball* and *fall* finds he or she can encode *call,* but to do this the child needs time to reflect and to be listened to and encouraged to look inside new words. With practice, young children unconsciously constantly use analogies to match sounds to spelling patterns. Making analogies increases self-confidence as it shows progress and also gives them the feeling that they are in control of their learning.

Through spelling quizzes a structured scheme of known spelling patterns can be consolidated and, where necessary, revision can be introduced. Quizzes also include a structured programme of puzzle words, stressing that these are special words that have to be learned by heart at this stage. As the selection of words with matching rimes increases, so does the child's range of vocabulary. Teachers need to support children by:

- creating quick sessions to search, discover and widen their recognition of patterns
- providing group of words with matching rimes but different onsets
- helping them find analogies
- explaining fun facts about words
- looking at the origins of words
- increasing vocabulary.

190

9.7 Learning new spellings

The 'look-cover-write-check' method of memorising spellings is used in many UK schools. This method provides children with a worksheet that encourages them to remember new spellings through observation of the word, memorising and finally writing from memory.

This 'look-cover-write-check' method is used for learning and testing the spelling of single words. However, when children are acquiring English as L2 it is more purposeful to include the word in spoken natural language (for example, with an article or in a short phrase: *a bike, an orange, a sunny day*). This will encourage children to transfer and include the words in their spoken and written language.

Teachers should only include known words for new spellings. They can include words which:

- have matching rimes: *small, fall, wall*
- appear in simple phrases: *a sunny day, a good* way
- appear in short sentences: *My red bag is there.*

How to use a 'look-cover-write-check' spelling sheet

Teachers can ask children to follow these steps:

Look: Look at the work in your book. Write the word in the air, or on the palm of your free hand with your index and middle finger.

Cover: Cover the word in your book. Close your eyes and see the word in your mind

Write: Open your eyes and write the word with your pencil.

Check: Uncover the word in your book and check. Do the spellings match?

Repeat: Do it again.

Figure 23 A spelling sheet

Look Say the letter names.	**Copy** Try writing the word. **Cover** Then cover it.	**Write** Write it. **Check** Is it right?	**Repeat** Now do it again.
cat			
hat			
bat			
mat			
fat			

↑
Teacher
writes the
words
or phrases

9.7.1 Puzzle words

When giving new spellings to the children, teachers should include one or two 'puzzle' (or 'sight') words to be memorised, to add some fun.

Puzzle words (also termed 'tricky' or 'key' words) have to be learned by sight as whole blocks during the period when children are learning to read. Without a selection of puzzle words children cannot complete written phrases and sentences to give meaning. As children become more competent readers many of these words will cease to be puzzle words, as children will be sufficiently skilled to analyse or partly analyse their letter patterns.

Example of important puzzle words are:

is   it   in   at   and   to   the   no   go   I   went   saw

9.7.2 Fun words and phrases

Additional phrases can be included in quizzes from time to time to give added variety and fun. These phrases play with sounds and need to be known as spoken language before they are introduced in quizzes. They provide fun opportunities to compare different ways to make sounds, and are likely to be memorised for life!

Examples of fun phrases:

A peach for each	*Any more, many more*
Sniff snuff smell	*Yes No – off you go*
Splish splash splosh	*Is it great to eat*
Never ever	*A busy bus*
Shark in the park in the dark	*Topsy Turvy*
Seven Eleven	*A nice slice of cake*

'Magic e' spellings (add an e and change the sound and the word):

Tim	*time*	*pin*	*pine*
can	*cane*	*hat*	*hate*
fir	*fire*	*hop*	*hope*
bit	*bite*	*fin*	*fine*
pip	*pipe*	*mad*	*made*

Rhyming words for numbers one to ten:

one: *fun, sun, run, gun, son, done*

two: *you, shoe, blue, glue, new, who*

three: *me, tree, bee, sea, pea, flea*

four: *door, more, store, sore*

five: *drive, hive, alive*

six: *mix, fix, kicks, licks, sticks*

seven: *eleven, heaven*

eight: *late, hate, date, gate*

nine: *line, fine, shine, mine*

ten: *men, hen, pen, again*

9.7.3 Today's word

Some schools introduce a new word in each lesson, accompanied by a quick, focused tutor-talk. The word is then displayed so children can see it throughout the lesson. At the end of the lesson the word is reviewed, together with other words that have been previously introduced as 'today's word'. Teachers can choose to focus in this way on words commonly misspelt by the class, for example.

9.8 Involving parents

Parents can be sources of valuable support if they feel positively about their child learning English and can see their progress. Once it has been explained to parents how they can help, their daily interest and support can contribute greatly to the child's 'feel-good factor' about English. Most want to be involved, although they might complain amongst themselves, saying things like *No more spelling tests this term, please!*

Some parents may assume their children find learning spellings stressful. However, those parents need to be helped to see the task through their children's eyes and emotions. Children are likely to have positive feelings about their spellings, providing the spelling quiz content is structured and administered with a playful approach into which the children can put in effort and succeed (see Chapter 3, page 61, Growth mindset). The spelling quiz routine gives children the feeling of acting like an adult, whilst also giving parents satisfaction that their child is learning.

Parents need to be kept informed and provided with explanations about how children learn spelling and how they can be supported. Parental support is very important for reinforcing their child's learning. The content of tutor-talks can be adapted for parents and sent to them by email, for example.

Parents may find some difficulty in pronouncing certain words and children will hasten to correct them. Explain to parents that this is in fact a good thing, as it shows that children can distinguish the sounds of words in spelling quizzes and know whether they are said correctly. It may also be possible to send recordings of the week's spellings to parents.

9.9 Fun facts

Think about spelling in a variety of ways, not least as a fascinating aspect of language.

(O'Sullivan in Dombey and Moustafa)

Spelling can be made fun by inserting interesting information about language that children can share with their parents. Teachers can build up a range of fun facts, collecting the sort of information that interests children and which can be included in a word quiz or group game. Such games can be run by the children with the teacher acting as the referee! This gives the teacher the opportunity to explain mistakes and fill in any answers.

Do you know …

- about double *ee*? Link them together and say them once. (*see, meet, green*) [Children can link arms to demonstrate]
- about double *oo*? It does not always say the same sound.
    - short *oo* (*cook, book, look, took, foot*)
    - long *oo* (*moon, zoo, food, cool, school, fool, loose*)
- about double consonants said as one letter? (*huff, puff, ball, call*)
- that *ck* sounds like *k*? (*lucky, duck, sack, stick, clock*)
- that you can speak French? You are speaking French when you say *croissant* and *pain au chocolat*.
- that some alphabet letters have two ways of saying their sound?
    - hard *c* (*cat, cow*) and soft *c* (*city, juice, nice, twice*)
    - hard *g* (*go, get, dog*) and soft *g* (*gentle, large, giraffe*)
- about two words in one? (*sunshine, seaweed, goldfish, watermelon*)
- about silent letters?
    - silent *k* (*knee, knot, know, knock, knife*)
    - silent *h* (*heir, hour*)
    - silent *w* (*write, wreck, wrist*)
    - silent *l* (*half, calf, chalk, talk*)
- how to say question words? *When, what, where, which* and *why* all start with a *w* sound – but not *who!* *Who* rhymes with *boo-hoo*.
- that a three-letter word can change what it means if you add a letter *e*? (*bit bite, pip pipe, hop hope, not note, us use, cub cube*)
- that no words end in the letter *v* in English? They always have an *e* at the end. (*gave, love, live, have*)
- that no words end in the letter *i* in English (apart from Italian words like *spaghetti, macaroni* and *taxi*)? Instead we use *y* at the end of words (*spy, fly, my*).

9.10 Introducing first grammar concepts

As an extension to fun facts about spelling, the teacher can begin to introduce simple grammar concepts. These will form a grammar foundation in preparation for a more analytical approach to learning English.

Homonyms

The word 'homonym' comes from the Greek word meaning 'similar name'. These words can:

- sound and look the same, but have different meanings: *bat* (animal) *bat* (cricket bat)
- sound the same, but have different spellings and meanings: *meat* (food) *meet* (verb)

Prefixes and Suffixes

The meaning of a word can be altered – or even changed completely – by adding a prefix before a root (base) word:

inter-net, no-where, re-turn, some-times, to-day, un-tidy, under-water, mis-take, in-correct.

Or by adding a suffix after a root word:

in-side, no-thing, some-where, no-where.

Past tense verbs

The letters *-ed* are added to the end of a regular verb root to show something has already happened. The spelling is the same for all regular verbs, but the pronunciation changes to either /t/, /d/ or /id/:

- *looked* /t/
- *played* /d/
- *wanted* /id/

9.11 Word origins

English is a vacuum-cleaner of a language. It sucks words
in from any language it makes contact with.

(Crystal)

According to David Crystal, English has borrowed words from over 350 languages around the world. Loan words come from contact between people and many originate from former British colonies, particularly where there was no equivalent English word to match a local concept or item.

The majority of loan words do not replace anything; in fact, they generally add a new dimension. Many loan words have been in English for generations, so people no longer think about their origins. Some even believe they were always English.

Young children are fascinated by the origin of loan words and some are proud to tell adults they speak some Hindi (*pyjamas*), Greek (*rhubarb*) and French (*button, herb, possible, beauty, gentle, croissant*).

Some words have come on a journey from Greek to Latin and then to French. When England was invaded and conquered by William of Normandy and his army in 1066, French became the spoken language of educated English people. At the beginning of the last century, French was still the official diplomatic language and English diplomats were therefore expected to speak it. This explains the prevalence of French loan words in English.

One of the difficulties caused by loan words is that their spelling does not always fit into the sound system of English. This is often the case with words that come from Greek, Latin and French.

Some loan words in English

Anorak Inuit language	*Safari* African languages
Banana Spanish	*City* French
Pyjamas Hindi	*Guitar* Spanish
Bazaar Turkish	*Curry* Tamil
Bungalow Hindi	*Soprano* Italian
Ski Norweigan	*Captain* Latin (*caput* = head)
Spaghetti Italian	*Telephone* Greek (*tele* = far, *phone* = sound/voice)

Children need to draw on a variety of strategies for spelling, sometimes within the same word. And this understanding needs to be reflected in teaching from the outset.

(O'Sullivan in Dombey and Moustafa)

All types of language practice should make sense to the child, as an activity and as meaningful language.

(Cameron)

The word is a shared territory; 'meaning' is an individually negotiated understanding.

(Halliday)

10

Projects and activities

10.1 Why projects and activities?

*Children develop their learning powers while being involved
in activities – and these activities can be opportunities to gain
more subject-specific skills and knowledge at the same time.*

(Stewart)

The value of projects and activities is not always clear to teachers until they have tried them. Once they have seen the passion it awakens in children, in some cases creating 'flow' experiences (see Chapter 1, page 24), they realise how much it can contribute to developing and consolidating children's self-educating strategies, self-esteem and identity.

*I got to know him as a different child. So much more was in
him that I didn't know about.*

(An English teacher)

Through working independently and also sharing and interacting with others, children teach and learn amongst themselves. They work out how to self-manage, organising and regulating what they do and how they learn.

For different reasons some children become frustrated and lose interest in learning English. Sometimes, however, the fresh aspect of working on a project can unexpectedly remotivate. Suddenly a child changes to be the one who knows the most about a subject and becomes newly respected by others. Motivation is precious and teachers need to foster children's hidden interests. In some cases it could be a family interest (which is often is the case with boys and sport, especially football).

*Children develop interest in things they think we are
interested in as they want to please us.*

(Bruce)

Through carefully selected projects and activities, it is possible to:

- introduce new language linked to the 'hidden syllabus'
- revise and consolidate new and known language
- develop own identity and culture in English
- foster holistic development
- foster use of specific self-strategies
- nurture critical and divergent thinking, leading to creativity and innovative ideas.

10.2 Selecting projects and activities

Initially it is important for teachers to select projects in which they themselves are interested, as enthusiasm is infectious. At the start, projects are generally teacher-led, based on the combined interests of the teacher and the children. Projects are usually successful as they include a playful approach, which arouses curiosity and gives children opportunities to think critically and show divergence.

Children's now greater maturity and English ability (both oral and written) widens the scope for projects and activities in which they can take part. The number of games included in the English programme diminishes as time goes on, since children now pick up language more easily and can therefore focus on projects and activities that stimulate cognitive development, as well as language acquisition.

Teachers still find it useful to have a selection of quick games ready for impromptu use at odd times (for example, when momentum has been lost, when a group has finished before the other groups, or when tidying up has been quicker than expected). Through quick games it is possible to rekindle interest and regain focus in a few minutes. As well as actual games, teacher can also draw on other activities with game-like qualities (for example, rhymes, jokes and tongue twisters).

10.2.1 Planning

While planning teachers have to remember that the process is still more important than the final product. Now children are more mature and independent, the process can be longer, stretching over two or more lessons. Projects may sometimes involve parents' support and their flexibility allows them to introduce more detailed information if children seem interested. Many children are logical thinkers and they need to feel that projects and activities have 'real' reasons to use English.

It is important not to underestimate children's ability to understand information, if the introduction is structured and interesting. They want to find out about the world and how the world works. Adults need to try to visualise through the children's eyes and respond to their questions with 'real' information; many children have already been round the world on screen.

Activities and projects need to be carefully planned to:

- start from children's approximate 'zone of proximal development' ('ZPD' – see Chapter 2, page 41)
- follow children's interests and develop them
- challenge children holistically
- provide a 'real' purpose to use English
- include experiences that enable children to think critically and creatively
- provide opportunities to work with others, brainstorming and sharing ideas.

Teacher also need to ensure the project or activity lasts an appropriate length of time, considering whether to:

- complete it in one, two or more lessons
- include a pre-lesson introduction (preparation)
- include a post-lesson summary (consolidation).

Without adequate opportunities to consolidate, children can acquire language, but not be able to use it effectively. Opportunities to consolidate orally and through reading and writing need to be planned into each stage. Records are evidence to children of their achievements and progress and are a way for teachers and parents to assess.

Consolidation can be done through making mini-books, putting on exhibitions, recording visually through photos, or recording orally on phones or tablets. Children like to revisit records, especially if they include photos. It gives them added opportunities to talk about what they did together, which is a natural way of consolidating. Teachers can also refer to exhibits in summing-up sessions at the end of lessons. Parents can be sent photos to their phones or by email, as this will create another talking point. Consolidation at home can take place in L1 or in English, as thinking in either language consolidates.

> *Projects gave him an opportunity to develop his own identity in the class and use his special knowledge of the names of fish and where they live in the sea.*
>
> (An English teacher)

Progress takes place through:

- modelling how to do the activity, accompanied by tutor-talk
- structuring activities or projects to make learning easier
- consolidating key teaching points
- including interactive sharing opportunities for teaching and learning together
- scaffolding language where necessary to recall or predict
- using open-ended questions to develop thinking.

Children may work in pairs or small groups, so that there are opportunities to learn from each other's different strategies and knowledge. Teachers need to move around the classroom, observing and interacting with children and keeping up a general commentary that can be heard by everyone. This way the teacher can orchestrate a rich language experience for the children.

Some activities and projects may not offer valuable learning opportunities because they:

- take too long to set up and children's interest has waned before they start
- are too difficult because they are way beyond children's zone of proximal development (ZPD) and level of interest
- are not sufficiently focused or structured and therefore waste learning time.

Some projects may be completed in one lesson, others can stretch over homework to the next lessons. Any continuation to be done as homework should be clearly explained beforehand so there is no confusion in children's minds. After working on something for two lessons, it may be difficult to keep up children's enthusiasm. Activities should change just before children begin to lose interest.

10.3 Parents' involvement

Keeping parents in the learning triangle means that children are in fact having extra tutorials. Parental support gives children confidence that they are going along the right track – a track of which their parents approve. Most parents enjoy this special way of supporting their children. Many also relish the opportunity to be involved again in a subject that may be taught very differently now from when they were at school.

To support children and projects parents need to understand the aims and how they can help. For many this way of working and supporting may be completely new. However, once parents feel children's enthusiasm they are generally eager to help, even if their help is limited to listening and giving words of encouragement. Parents often find they can learn from their children and sometimes their children enjoy teaching *them*, playing the role of the English teacher!

Parents need to understand that learning English means being able to communicate about something 'real' and that this is what projects and activities enable children to do. If parents talk about the content of projects (either in LI or it English) it often turns into a bonding experience. It means, however, that the teacher must be ready to welcome any information in LI and then recast that information in English. Alternatively, the teacher can introduce relevant English vocabulary in the preparation phase of the project or activity. This vocabulary can even be supplied to parents along with a brief outline of the project or activity. There is no need to worry about parents pronouncing the words with a foreign accent, as children can use different accents when and where needed and still know that the teacher's pronunciation is the model to copy.

Parents have expertise and most want to help. Invite them to see progress or ask them to recommend YouTube videos relevant to project, or even to make their own recordings. They can also collect pictures and other materials, but if possible give them plenty of time to search as working parents are often very busy.

10.4 Suggested projects or activities

Children learning English need to be able to talk about their own identity in English. They need to understand their identity does not change when they speak English – they are still the same person. It is only the language that changes, not the content.

It is good, however, to prepare children to talk about themselves in English so they do not feel overwhelmed if they meet an English-speaking person (for example, on an international holiday, or if an international visitor comes to the school). Children need to realise that they need English to talk in and to the world.

10.4.1 Project 1: Me, my town, my country

Preparation

<u>Interview game</u>

The teacher uses a microphone (fake or real) to conduct mini-interviews with children:

Teacher:	*Hello. What's your name? Your first name.*
Child:	*It's Beth.*
Teacher:	*Hello, Beth. And what's your family name?*
Child:	*Gonzalez.*
Teacher:	*This is Beth Gonzalez, everyone!*

The child being interviewed then takes the microphone and chooses another child to inteview, and so on round the class. The interviewer's language can be adapted as the activity progresses, for example:

Interviewer:	*Hello, Anna. How old are you?*
Anna:	*Seven years old.*
Interviewer:	*When's your birthday?*
Anna:	*In February.*
Interviewer:	*Where do you live?*
Anna:	*I live in [town]. It's in [country].*

<u>Birthday game</u>

The teacher says *Tell me when your Birthday is. It it January? February?* etc. Children stand up when they hear their birthday month. The teacher repeats the activity more quickly, asking children to recite the months too, until all children can recite the months.

<u>Homework</u>

The teacher asks children to do the following:

Write your first name in CAPITALS.

Write your surname in CAPITALS.

Put a cross by your birthday month. [The teacher supplies a calendar or a list of months for this.]

Project

The teacher distributes copies of the script below. He or she reads the script aloud, with the children following. There are blanks for personal information. In pairs children interview each other, reading or memorising the script.

Interviewer: *Good morning . Today I am at .... School. Hello everyone.*

Interviewer: *What's your name? Your first name .*

Interviewee: *...............*

Interviewer: *Hello .... And what's your family name?*

Interviewee: *...............*

Interviewer: *How old are you?*

Interviewee: *......... years old.*

Interviewer: *When's your birthday?*

Interviewee: *In ....*

Interviewer: *Where do you live?*

Interviewee: *I live in ....*

Interviewer: *Thank you .... Goodbye.*

<u>Homework</u>

The teacher asks children to complete the blanks in the script. Children can also draw and colour their national flag, or interview members of their family using a home-made microphone.

10.4.2 Project 2: My identity card

Preparation

The teacher talks to the children about the reasons for making their own identity card. The teacher also prepares blank identity cards to be taken home and discussed with parents. Children and parents can discuss if/ when capital letters should be used to complete the cards, and what information should be included. They can use the guide questions provided. They can write rough answers together, and perhaps draw their national flag to illustrate the card.

Identity Card information:

First name ....

Family name ....

Birthday month ....

Town / Country ....

School name..................................

Head Teacher's name ....

English Teacher's name ....

Signature ....

[insert photo]

Guide questions in English

What is your first name?

What is your family name?

When were you born?

Where do you live?

What is the name of your school?

What is the name of the Head Teacher?

What is the name of your English Teacher?

Project

The teacher checks the rough answers with the class, getting children to self-correct if necessary. The completed identity cards can be printed or copied onto card, coloured in and displayed.

10.4.3 Project 3: Our festivals

Local festivals are important occasions for young children and they often want to be able to talk about them in English. However, the necessary vocabulary is rarely found in books suitable for young beginners. For this reason it is advisable for teachers to make material together with the children. It is a good opportunity for children to realise that local festivals may also have names in English, or that it is acceptable to code-switch local names into English phrases. If there are games related to local festivals, they can be played using English. Making a photo book about typical food eaten at a festival can make an interesting addition to the book corner.

10.4.4 Project 4: A compass

Preparation

The teacher shows a compass to the class and explains about the North and the North Pole. Children identify the four points of the compass, saying *This is the North* etc. The teacher can also introduce the following rhyme:

North, South, East and West
Home is best.

Activity

<u>Compass game</u>

The teacher points out North, South, East and West in the classroom. He or she then says *Turn to the South, Turn to the North,* etc. Children have to follow the instructions and anyone who makes a mistake drops out.

<u>Homework</u>

The teacher prints two copies of the compass rhyme above for each child. One of the copies is cut into words. At home, children order the words to match them to the complete rhyme. Children can also ask their parents *Where is the South? Where is the North?* etc.

<u>Follow up</u>

The compass activity can lead on to other questions like *Where does the sun rise? Where does the sun set? The sun rises in the East. The sun sets in the West.*

10.4.5 Project 5: My map

This project involves looking at printed and/or online maps, such as Google Maps. The children have opportunities to compare different maps and photographs.

Preparation

The children look at one or more maps of their local area. They choose their favourite map and, with their parents' help, draw the route they take from home to school.

Project

In class, the children complete some text to go with their map, following the template below. Teachers might need to introduce telling the time in English or using the international clock.

How I get to school

Here is my home and here is my school. This red line shows my way to school.

I come to school by bicycle/scooter/bus/car.

I walk to school.

I leave home at . . . .

I get to school at . . . .

Figure 24 My map

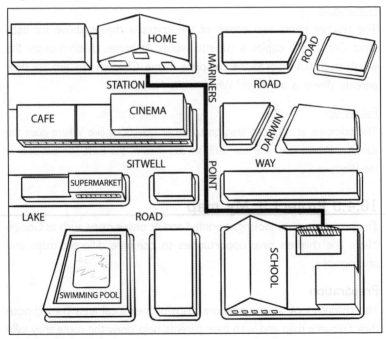

Follow up

After using local maps, children can move on to country maps. They can identify their home town as well as other towns, cities, countries and continents.

10.4.6 Project 6: The auto show

This is a project based on commercial advertising for world auto shows.

Preparation

The teacher introduces the concept of an auto show, telling children a catchy slogan like:

The Auto Show – You've got to go!

At home, the children look for and collect coloured images of the latest models of cars, cutting them out or printing them. They can also collect:

- the names of the car companies (*Honda, Rolls Royce, Audi,* etc.)
- any advertising slogans in English
- details of the different types of car (hybrid, electric, etc.)
- details of the fastest car, the most expensive car, etc.

Project

Each child or group of children chooses their favourite car for the auto show. They mount a picture of their favourite car on paper and together label the parts of the car, outside as well as inside, if possible. Advertisements on the Internet can help with sourcing the appropriate terminology. The teacher helps children find out where the car is made or assembled. The teacher can then co-build an imaginary story with the children about the car's first or longest journey.

Children can also say sentences like these about the cars at the auto show:

If I could choose any car, I would buy a .... [name of the car]
If my Dad could choose, he would buy a ....
If my Mum could choose, she would buy a ....

10.4.7 Project 7: Making a card

Giving greeting cards is very popular and making a card for an extended member of the family can give pleasure and show that children care.

Preparation

The teacher introduces the idea behind greeting cards and discusses when and why we give them (for example, for festivals, birthdays or holidays).

Activity

The teacher presents two different ways to make a card and the children have to select one way by thinking critically. (Different types of card design can be found easily online.) The teacher prepares coloured card of the appropriate size and models the two ways to make the cards, according to the instructions found online.

The children make their own card and decide where and what to write in it. The teacher can provide a selection of texts for children to choose from and copy. They then add their signature with their name printed underneath, using a capital letter followed by small letters.

10.4.8 Project 8: Exhibition day

Young children between the ages of 6 and 8 are sometimes passionate collectors. Their collections might be of shells, stamps or things they have made like origami (folded paper animals and objects). It is interesting for teachers and other children to know about their collections, many of which are too big to introduce in a 'My secret' session (see Chapter 6, page 97).

Holding a special 'Exhibition day' can be very special for some children as it gives them an opportunity to show off their knowledge of their particular hobby.

Teachers need to introduce each collection in English to the other children, giving a type of tutor-talk about its content. The teacher has to be ready to help children label their collection in English as well as in L1, so that it is clear there are two ways to say the same thing. The teacher needs to orchestrate the arrangement of the exhibition but the management of the guests can be the responsibility of the children.

The children can invite other classes to come and see the exhibition by sending invitations or making posters, which are put up round the school. Children will learn from seeing and talking amongst each other, and seeing other children's enthusiasm for collecting can be infectious.

Figure 25 A class exhibition poster

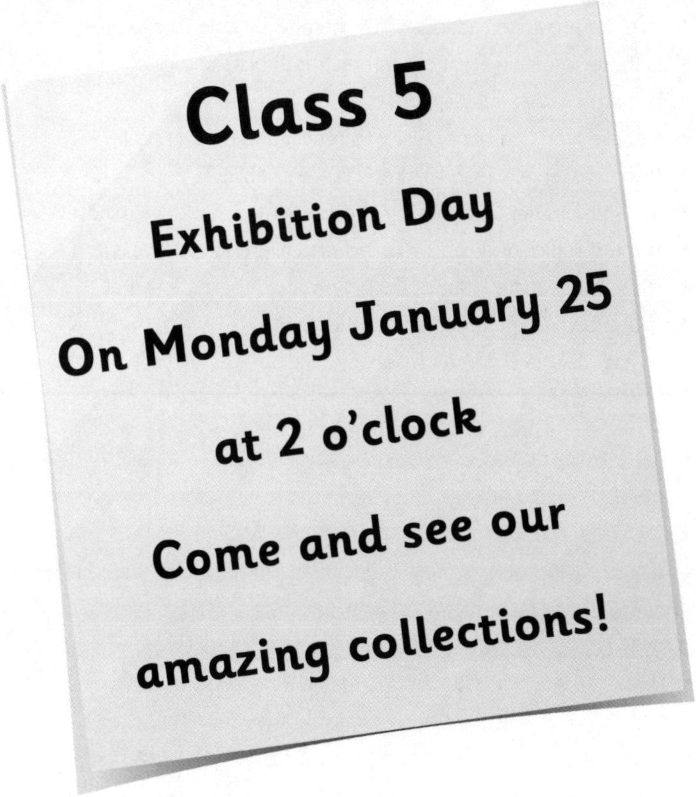

Class 5

Exhibition Day

On Monday January 25

at 2 o'clock

Come and see our

amazing collections!

10.5 Assessing

Here are some points to consider when monitoring and assessing project work:

- Are the children all actively engaged?
- Are the provisions adequate for them to be able to explore?
- Is there something that can interest both boys and girls?
- Is there enough adult support?
- Is there time and opportunity to reflect and think critically?
- Is the challenge within children's range of ability?
- Will the project be appealing and encourage a positive mindset?
- Is there sufficient flexibility to include children's initiative?
- Is there adequate input of English or could there be more?
- Is the follow-up focused and motivating?
- What was the children's reaction?

11

Enjoying reading and writing creatively

11.1 Attitudes to creative writing and reading

Reading books is only part of enjoying them. Making books is also learning.

(An English teacher)

Cultures differ in their attitudes to the place of creativity in education. If there is no place for creative writing in LI, the teacher's introduction should be gradual, firstly helping the child to think creatively and showing how innovative ideas are welcome. If creative thinking and writing is valued in LI, the teacher has to find out how to reuse the existing LI strategies in English.

In many classrooms the method of instruction (teacher-led) is not conducive to working creatively. In other classrooms, where children are being prepared for tests, there is no time or place for creative activities, even reading for pleasure.

Writing creatively depends on spoken ability and both depend on experience in LI and English – especially creative experiences in reading illustrated books and being involved in projects and activities that require reading, critical thinking and decision making. It is not easy for many native speakers to begin to write creatively. Teachers often use oral reporting of news or descriptions as the bridge to real creative writing.

Creative writing is a big leap for children who are not encouraged to read for pleasure or to write on paper – either at home or at school. No wonder children ask teachers to help them. Teachers should not push children to achieve too much at this stage of development, but be content to sow the seeds by making sure children know how to use their self-learning strategies when they are ready.

Creative writing needs to have a purpose. Who is it for? To create a text in a notebook and then simply have the teacher correct the spelling with a red pencil is not going to motivate creative writing. A purpose children can understand at this age is writing books. Published books can be in the classroom book corner for everyone to read. Books are something children know about as they are reading books all the time; creating text to make books is natural progress.

However, creativity should not be pushed. Any modelling and scaffolding should not be so imposing that the child does not get the glow of satisfaction from having created something. A creation is neither right nor wrong. Any criticism can limit willingness on the part of the child to take a risk to create in the future, as the child might fear that the output will be classed as 'wrong' or not meet the teacher's vision. Children of lower-primary age still want to please the teacher.

11.2 Starting from the child's ideas

In the beginning of creative writing and reading children need support, openly asking for it by saying things like *Show me how. Do it with me.* To be able to offer structured help starting from children's approximate 'zone of proximal development' ('ZPD' – see Chapter 2, page 41), the teacher has to understand:

* the types of experience gained in L1 (teacher-led and social)
* local cultural attitudes to creativity (value of spoken ideas and creative writing, including stories, rhymes, songs)
* the types of screen exposures children have out of school
* the children's experience with presenting and talking aloud in class ('My secret' sessions)
* the scaffolding support children are used to receiving in spoken English to describe and narrate.

One teacher described the following incident, which reveals local attitudes to creativity:

For the dolls' festival children were given doll outlines and told to add features. Since local dolls are traditional with fixed features, children added only what they had previously observed. There was no room in their minds for creativity. The result was that their artwork all looked more or less the same, the differences only being noticeable in the chidren's colouring skills.

As children's oral fluency increases, more language is transferred as whole or part phrases. Children have also acquired an ability to rearrange words in phrases and recast language to *I* from *she* or *he*. Range of language function has also increased as most children can use – without thinking how language works – simple forms of:

- identifying language
- descriptive language
- narrative language (past and predicting)
- conversation and commands (management language)
- reported speech.

Initially most transferred language is generally identification and management language, or narrative (explaining past adventures). Descriptive language tends to need extra scaffolding help.

11.3 Modelling and scaffolding

Teachers rarely meet children who can initiate their own stories or other creative writing without guidance and support. Most children cannot visualise how to make the bridge between short picture books to writing their own creative texts. To be faced with a blank piece of paper and be told to describe a dog, for example, can be overwhelming and demotivating.

Children know about books, so writing and illustrating their own stories or information books is a concept they understand that has a 'real' purpose (see Chapter 7, page 132, Little books). A book can provide a known scaffold sequence on which to hang written creative language.

Modelling how to make a simple book, with accompanying step-by-step explanations, can be exciting. Children can make a cover for their book too, using thicker, coloured paper. Making the book can come before the content, which can begin to be developed whilst the book is being made. First books should be short. They should contain simple text and not be overambitious, as they need to be successful if they are to lead on to others.

Before making books, the teacher should co-share by looking at short books composed of five spreads or so. The teacher can also look at the title pages and covers of bigger books. Talking about how books are written and illustrated may be new to some children.

The next step is to make a storyboard, laying out the pages (sequencing) so the child can see where to place the text and where to fit the illustrations.

Figure 26 A storyboard

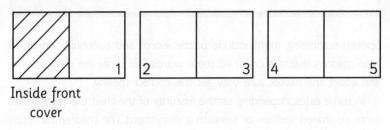

Inside front
cover

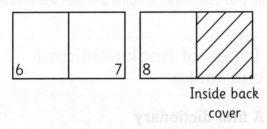

Inside back
cover

The teacher should scaffold the co-sharing of ideas to help children come up with content for their books. Selecting the title may well be the last step of content creation, as titles are usually a summary of the story! All ideas should be talked through in a type of brainstorming before focusing on the activity, with scaffolding led by the teacher and more able children.

Forms of scaffolding are now more complex as the child has his or her own ideas. In many cases, the child may in fact lead the scaffolding. The teacher should act as an editor, while the children are the authors.

Scaffolding can include the following elements:

- Talking about introductions and endings
- Talking about content
- Providing scaffolding props (see 11.4.4)
- Co-creating text and fitting it to pages
- Co-creating and deciding on a title
- Adding the name of the author and/or illustrator

Spoken scaffolding might include puzzle words and continuity words. To help children, teachers could list these words. This saves the children time and effort and makes sure they get the correct spelling.

In some cases, depending on the maturity of the child, the teacher can write co-shared text on or beneath a storyboard. The children can copy the text into their own books at home and then add illustrations.

11.4 Types of books children can make

11.4.1 A first dictionary

Making a first dictionary is a useful activity for:

- introducing how to use a dictionary
- consolidating awareness of 'onset'
- introducing some basic grammar
- providing a reference book for checking spellings
- creating further opportunities for tutor-talks.

Children need a plain notebook, allowing a single page for each letter of the alphabet. Entries can be made in one or two columns on each page, depending on the space available. At this stage children should enter words according to their first letter only (words do not need to be in alphabetical order within each page).

Children can begin by entering the first 12 puzzle words (six in one lesson, and six in the next). They can then continue entering the next 20 puzzle words over four further lessons (five each time). Dictionary entry work can be a homework task.

On the back pages of the dictionary, leave room for important grammar points already introduced through tutor-talk linked to spelling quizzes. Teachers need to focus on some of the differences between L1 and English when introducing grammar. Children are now beginning to develop critical thinking and analytic strategies to compare language content. Here are some points that could be covered:

- Time words to express past and future (*today, tomorrow*)
- Use of pronouns or special words to show family relationships and hierarchy (*older sister, younger brother*)
- Systems to make plurals
- Use of capital letters
- Use of comma, speech marks, question marks and exclamation marks

Children can look for and discuss examples of punctuation in real books. In creative writing at this stage, teachers should only expect children to use:

- a capital letter at the beginning of a sentence
- a full stop at the end of a sentence
- speech marks for direct speech.

11.4.2 Illustrated books

Children who find illustrating difficult can be encouraged to decorate their books by sticking in characters from magazines, for example. The cut-out images can be embellished with further detail by the children. Speech bubbles can also be added, recording what a character says or thinks.

Other children may want to illustrate their books with photos taken on smartphones. All possibilities should be encouraged as they will help to build the bridge to creative thought.

11.4.3 Superheroes and superheroines

Superheroes are not just a childhood phenomenon. Comics about them are also read by adults, and not exclusively men! This is nothing new; Greek myths were about superheroes, too. Superheroes (and heroines) have the ability to captivate children's imaginations, especially boys. They often represent 'goodies' trying to overcome 'baddies' (binary opposites) and take part in risk-taking episodes that always end happily. Children feel reassured by this narrative pattern. Being superheroes gives children the feeling of being in control of their world, which, in reality, they are not. Expressing feelings about superheroes through making a book can help children, especially boys, manage their emotions and develop self-control.

Children have their own ideas about superheroes and superheroines and writing about one can be a very important experience for them. Teachers can copy pictures of the characters and use them as a base for a story or a report in book form. Speech bubbles can be added to animate the images.

11.4.4 Monsters faces

This book-making activity involves talking about and drawing monsters.

- Children are given a large piece of paper folded in two to make a booklet, and crayons. On the title page of the booklet the teacher or the children can write *My Three Monsters.*
- The teacher checks that children know the words for parts of the face, making a list as a scaffold prop.
- Children discuss what their monsters' faces might look like, stimulated by the teacher's self-talk: *Does my monster have three or four arms? I wonder if his mouth is open or shut.*
- Children draw a monster face on page one of their booklet, and label the parts of the face. Underneath the monster they write *The best Monster.*
- The teacher circulates, encouraging individuals and pairs and giving a commentary to the class.
- All the monster booklets are exhibited. During the exhibition, each child explains one feature of their monster's face.
- Children then draw a second but different monster's face (*The worst Monster*), again labelling, exhibiting and describing it.
- For homework children draw their third monster on the back page of the booklet, calling it *A baby monster.* In the next lesson, children talk about their baby monster.

This framework can be used to describe many other things. The teacher should aim to gradually diminishing the picture element and increase the amount of text.

11.5 Towards fluent reading

Recreational reading is the most powerful tool available for language and literacy development. It is especially important for helping second and foreign language acquirers develop the ability to use language for more than simple conversation. The amount of pleasure from reading done in the second language is a strong predictor of performance in tests of writing, reading, grammar and vocabulary.

(Krashen)

Fluent reading is not only about how well you can decode words. It is also about reading for pleasure, as well as reading to stimulate your mind and help you think critically. Above all, reading should be an enjoyable and interesting experience shared by the teacher with his or her children, and by parents with their children. Reading helps the reader to immerse themselves in the ideas, thoughts and dreams of others.

As children grow in confidence and have more diverse experiences, their skills in orchestrating their decoding strategies increase and become more refined. Like adults, they unconsciously decode a word and read it. If you ask them how they decoded it, they may find difficulty in explaining.

Learning to read continues to develop through reading and most especially reading real books. Through reading illustrated books children are naturally exposed to various genres of language. They are finding out how language works. By this age children are not only wanting to read stories but also information books. Apart from having opportunities to book browse, children need opportunities to co-share books with a teacher who continues to source, provide and mediate new books.

By now scaffolding based on an illustrated book has deepened and is more challenging. Scaffolding has developed from identifying and discussing what is on the page (*What colour is the ...? What's the dog doing?*) to predicting and analysing (*What will he do? Can the girl help? Will he get there on time?*). Scaffolding also now covers recapping, analysing and personalising (*Do you remember what he did? Why do you think she did that? Do you think he was right to do that?*).

11.5.1 Developing reading skills

Skill in reading, like all skills, takes time to develop and can only do so when learners are given many varied opportunities to read. Ideally, therefore, young children should find themselves in a reading-rich environment. This means that, in addition to textbooks, children should have the chance to read some of the print around them in everyday life (for example, posters, magazines and packaging), as well as having opportunities to borrow all kinds of books (stories, rhymes, reference books, etc.).

Silent reading (Aural Reading)

Most children have now got to the stage where they do not need to read aloud to themselves: they read silently 'in their head'.

Reading aloud (Oral Reading)

Reading aloud is a different skill from silent reading. As reading skills become more fluent, children need opportunities to experiment with both. However, not too much importance should be put on reading aloud in a group, especially from a textbook or reader, unless there is a definite purpose. Reading aloud is not a skill many adults use regularly.

Children should never be expected to read aloud any material they have not already encountered. Teachers need to be wary of attaching too much importance to reading aloud as there is a danger that children will start scanning the text to match the speed of their speech. In fact, efficient silent reading should be at a much faster pace than reading aloud.

However, young children appear to enjoy reading aloud and get great satisfaction from it, especially when reading to their teacher. They continually ask when it is their turn and are disappointed if they do not get a chance in every lesson. Reading aloud to the teacher also gives children an added opportunity to have personal contact with the teacher, and enables the teacher to hear any mistakes and assess the child's decoding techniques. The teacher might say things like *Let's read this book together. I like the picture on the cover. What do you think it tells us about? Let me hear you read. Start from the first paragraph on the last page.* Self-recording on a phone or tablet is fun and gives children opportunities to hear their mistakes and self-correct, if given time.

Children learn from imitating and if they are to read well aloud it is necessary for them to hear a good model of reading. Models can be either the teacher reading or recordings on YouTube. Children soon learn to read with expression and vary their voices to portray characters or create atmosphere.

Copying reading (Visual reading)

Copying consolidates reading and opportunities for copying should be given for homework. Children can copy texts from their storybooks or rhyme books, adding their own illustrations. This gives them opportunities to be creative and show the teacher the depth of their understanding of the text. Copying may seem boring to adults but to some children it is important. It seems to give them a feeling of being in control and knowing a lot of English.

Correcting Mistakes

Decoding is complex and naturally children make mistakes. Often teachers and other eager children in the group supply the correct reading before the reader has had time to reflect. If children are to have opportunities to work out how to self-correct using their own multi-strategies, they need time. Teachers need to explain this to other children as their eagerness to be helpful in correcting can dent a slow reader's self-esteem.

11.5.2 The book corner

A book corner is still important in the classroom though its role may now have changed to be also an exhibition centre, with a pin board and table for exhibits. Ideally it should house at least one real book per child as well as some reference books, including dictionaries and information books.

A borrowing card can be placed in a small envelope at the back of a book. These provide a useful record of who has borrowed each book.

As the purpose of the book corner has increased to also house exhibitions, two children should now share the associated responsibilities, one acting as the Librarian and the other the Curator.

Duties of the book corner Librarian:

- Keep the book corner tidy.
- Check that borrowed books are returned.
- Organise space for book browsing.

Duties of the exhibition centre Curator:

- Make sure that exhibits are returned to their owners.
- Make labels for exhibits.
- Organise space for exhibition browsing.

The teacher has to model where necessary, showing how to manage effectively, whilst encouraging children to visit the exhibitions and borrow real books. Real books can inspire children to write their own books. It is quite common for books made by children to be adaptations of real books, or to be inspired by real books.

> *Literature provides meaning in our lives. Finding of meaning is the greatest need and the most difficult achievement for any human of our age.*

> (Bettelheim)

Final thoughts

> *Creative thinking is not a talent; it is a skill that can be learned. It empowers people by adding strength to their natural abilities.*
>
> (de Bono)

By now, young children learning English as a second or third language are already aware that some problems can be solved in two different ways to give one answer. Often these discoveries are made first with numbers in both a first language and in English. Although each numeral is generally written the same way, each number has two different names.

Unlike monolingual children, whose thinking is linear, these children are unconsciously developing skills to think laterally. To make a choice involves critical thinking: *Which one?* The decision links with creativity to complete a creative process. In an English class, with a sensitive teacher who arouses curiosity and values new ideas, this can lead to innovation. These are the seeds of life-long abilities to create and innovate.

Sincerely,

Opal Dunn —

List of terminology

Child–parent–teacher triangle defines the cooperative liaison routes for effective and holistic individual child development.

Homonym comes from a Greek word meaning 'similar name' and refers to words which look and/or sound the same but have different spellings and/or meanings.

L1 refers to the first or home language.

L2 is the term used where English is the second new language.

Loan words develop from contact between peoples and many originate from where there was no equivalent English word to match a local concept or item.

Onset consists of all the letters and phonemes (blends, diagraphs) which appear *before* the first vowel in a word: b/oat, tr/ain, pl/ay.

Prefixes can alter or change meaning when added before the root (base) of a word: *inter*-net, *no*-where, *re*-turn.

Puzzle words (also termed 'tricky' or 'key' words) have to be learned by sight as whole blocks during the initial period when children are learning to read.

Rime continues from the first vowel of a word to the end of the word. Through rime the patterns in words are clearly identified and children can hear and see them more easily: t/*able*, st/*able*, p/*air*, st/*air*, b/*oat*, g/*oat*.

Show and tell / My secret is a session included within circle times which provides children with an opportunity to introduce something special from home to the class.

Suffixes can alter or change meaning when added after the root (base) of a word: in-*side*, no-*thing*.

Syllables are made up of phonemes and are the phonological building blocks of words.

Transition describes the changes incurred by moving between schooling levels throughout compulsory education.

ZPD (zone of proximal development) was defined by Lev Vygotsky as the gap between what children can do on their own without help and what they can achieve with assistance from an adult or more able child.

References and further reading

Barrs, M, Bromley, H, Dombey, H, Ellis, S, Kelly, C and Moustafa, M (1998) *Whole to Part Phonics: How Children Learn to Read and Spell.* London: Heinemann

Bettelheim, B (1991) *The Uses of Enchantment.* (4th ed). London: Penguin

Blissett, C and Hallgarten, K (1985) *A Very Simple Grammar of English.* Language Teaching Publications

Bronowski, J (1991) *The Ascent of Man.* New York: Little Brown

Bruce, T (1987) *Early Childhood Education.* London: Hodder and Stoughton

Bruce, T (1991) *Time to Play in Early Childhood Education.* London: Hodder and Stoughton

Bruner, J S (1972) 'Nature and Uses of Immaturity', American Psychologist, Vol. 27, No. 8

Bruner, J S (1974) 'Child's Play', New Scientist, 62, 126

Bruner, J S, Jolly, A and Sylva, K (1976) *Play: Its Role in Development and Evolution.* New York: Penguin

Bruner, J S (1996) *The Culture of Education.* Harvard: Harvard University Press

Cameron, L (2001) *Teaching Languages to Young Learners.* Cambridge: Cambridge University Press

Claxton, G (2006) 'Expanding the capacity to learn: A new end for education?', British Educational Research Association Annual Conference, Warwick University, 6th September 2006

Clay, M (1983) *Reading Recovery: A Guide Book for Teachers in Training.* Heinemann Education

Crystal, D (2012) *The Story of English in 100 Words.* London: Profile Books

Crystal, D (2006) *Words, Words, Words.* Oxford: Oxford University Press

Crystal, D (1989) *Listen to Your Child: A Parent's Guide to Children's Language.* London: Penguin Books

Csikszentmihalyi, M (1990) *The Psychology of Optimal Experience.* New York: Harper and Row de Bono, E (2014) 'Lateral Thinking Workshop', EdwdeBono: http://edwdebono.com/debono/worklt.htm (April 2014)

Dombey, H and Moustafa, M (1998) *Whole to Part Phonics: How Children Learn to Read and Spell.* London: Centre for Language in Primary Education

Dombey, H (2006) 'How Should We Teach Our Children to Read?', Books for Keeps: http://booksforkeeps.co.uk/issue/156/childrens-books/articles/other-articles/how-should-we-teach-children-to-read (April 2014)

Dweck, C (2006) *Mindset: The new Psychology of Success.* Random House

Engel, L (2013) 'EYFS Best Practice: All about Teaching in the EYFS', http://www.nurseryworld.co.uk/nursery-world/feature/1139742/eyfs-practice-about-teaching-eyfs (October 2013)

Foster, J (2004) *First Rhyming Dictionary.* Oxford: Oxford University Press

Garfield, A (2007) *Phonics the Easy Way.* London: Vermilion

Goleman, D (2009) *Emotional Intelligence.* New York: Random House

Goleman, D (2013) *Focus: The Hidden Driver of Excellence.* Bloomsbury

Goswami, U and Bryant, P (1990) *Phonological Skills and Learning to Read.* New Jersey: Lawrence Erlbaum Associates

Halliday, M (1975) *Learning How to Mean: Explorations in the Development of Language.* London: Edward Arnold

Harding, E and Philip, R (1986) *The Bilingual Family.* Cambridge: Cambridge University Press

Hunt, R and Hepplewhite, D (2013) *Oxford Phonics Spelling Dictionary (Oxford Reading Tree).* Oxford: Oxford University Press

Krashen, S (1981) *Second Language Acquisition and Second Language Learning.* Oxford: Pergamon Institute of English

Krashen, S (2004) *The Power of Reading.* Oxford: Heinemann

Layard, R (2006) *Happiness Lessons from a New Science.* Penguin Books

McWilliam, N (1998) *What's in a Word?: Vocabulary Development in Multi-Lingual Classrooms.* Staffordshire: Trentham Books

Michelin Maps and Guides (2009) *I-Spy Guides.* Michelin

Moyles, J (1989) *Just Playing: The Role and Status of Play in Early Education.* Open University Press

Pound L and Hughes C (2005) *How Children Learn: From Montessori to Vygotsky - Educational Theories and Approaches Made Easy,* Step Forward Publishing

Primary National Strategy (2007) *Letters and Sounds: Principles and Practice of High Quality Phonics.* London: Department for Education and Skills

Rosen, M (2013) 'To the point. Do you read me?', Nursery World, 28th January to 10th February 2013

Sassoon, R (1995) *The Acquisition of a Second Writing Script.* London: Intellect Books

Smith, S 'Onset and Rime', Crossbow Education: http://www.crossboweducation.com/articles/onset-and-rime-(analytic-phonics)/ (April 2014)

Stewart, N (2011) *How children learn – The Characteristics of Effective Early Learning.* London: Early Education Publishers

Taeschner, T (2005) *Learning a Foreign Language at Nursery School.* CILT Publications

Tough, P (2013) *How Children Succeed.* Random House

Ticknell, C (2011) *The Early Years Foundations for Life.* Department for Education

Whitehead, M R (2002) *Developing Language and Literature with Young Children.* Peter Chapman Publishing

Wylie, R E and Durrell, D D (1970) 'Teaching vowels through phonograms', Elementary English, 147, 789–91

Appendix

Letter formation with flick

a b c d e

f g h i j k

l m n o p

q r s t u

v w x y z

The table on the opposite page lists the next 200 common words in order of frequency, following on from the 100 high-frequency words table on page 124.

The list is read down in columns with **water** being the most frequently used word and **grow** being the least frequently used word.

The table is taken from: Masterson, J., Stuart, M., Dixon, M. and Lovejoy, S. (2003) Children's Printed Word Database: Economic and Social Research Council funded project, R00023406.

Next 200 common words in order of frequency

water	find	live	fun	better
away	more	say	place	hot
good	I'll	soon	mother	sun
want	round	night	sat	across
over	tree	narrator	boat	gone
how	magic	small	window	hard
did	shouted	car	sleep	floppy
man	us	couldn't	feet	really
going	other	three	morning	wind
where	food	head	queen	wish
would	fox	king	each	eggs
or	through	town	book	once
took	way	I've	its	please
school	been	around	green	thing
think	stop	every	different	stopped
home	must	garden	let	ever
who	red	fast	girl	miss
didn't	door	only	which	most
ran	right	many	inside	cold
know	sea	laughed	run	park
bear	these	let's	any	lived
can't	began	much	under	birds
again	boy	suddenly	hat	duck
cat	animals	told	snow	horse
long	never	another	air	rabbit
things	next	great	trees	white
new	first	why	bad	coming
after	work	cried	tea	he's
wanted	lots	keep	top	river
eat	need	room	eyes	liked
everyone	that's	last	fell	giant
our	baby	jumped	friends	looks
two	fish	because	box	use
has	gave	even	dark	along
yes	mouse	am	grandad	plants
play	something	before	there's	dragon
take	bed	gran	looking	pulled
thought	may	clothes	end	we're
dog	still	tell	than	fly
well	found	key	best	grow

Spelling sheet

Look Say the letter names.	**Copy** Try writing the word. **Cover** Then cover it.	**Write** Write it. **Check** Is it right?	**Repeat** Now do it again.

Letters and sounds: Principles and practice of high quality phonics notes of guidance for practitioners and teachers

Tables 1 to 4: The representation of phonemes

Table 1: Phonemes to graphemes (consonants)

Phoneme	Correspondences found in many different words		High-frequency words containing rare or unique correspondences (graphemes are underlined)
	Grapheme(s)	Sample words	
/b/	b, bb	bat, rabbit	
/k/	c, k, ck	cat, kit, duck	s<u>ch</u>ool, mos<u>qu</u>ito
/d/	d, dd, -ed	dog, muddy, pulled	
/f/	f, ff, ph	fan, puff, photo	rou<u>gh</u>
/g/	g, gg	go, bigger	
/h/	h	hen	<u>wh</u>o
/j/	j, g, dg	jet, giant, badge	
/l/	l, ll	leg, bell	
/m/	m, mm	map, hammer	la<u>mb</u>, autu<u>mn</u>
/n/	n, nn	net, funny	<u>gn</u>at, <u>kn</u>ock
/p/	p, pp	pen, happy	
/r/	r, rr	rat, carrot	<u>wr</u>ite, <u>rh</u>yme
/s/	s, ss, c	sun, miss, cell	<u>sc</u>ent, li<u>st</u>en
/t/	t, tt, -ed	tap, butter, jumped	<u>Th</u>omas, doub<u>t</u>
/v/	v	van	o<u>f</u>
/w/	w	wig	peng<u>u</u>in, *one*
/y/	y	yes	on<u>i</u>on
/z/	z, zz s, se, ze	zip, buzz, is, please, breeze	sci<u>ss</u>ors, <u>x</u>ylophone
/sh/	sh, s, ss, t (before -ion and -ial)	shop, sure, mission, mention, partial	spe<u>ci</u>al, <u>ch</u>ef, o<u>ce</u>an
/ch/	ch, tch	chip, catch	
/th/	th	thin	
/th/	th	then	brea<u>the</u>
/ng/	ng, n (before k)	ring, pink	ton<u>gue</u>
/zh/	s (before -ion and -ure)	vision, measure	u<u>su</u>al, bei<u>ge</u>

In the last column words printed in italic are from the list of 100 words occurring most frequently in children's books.

Table 2: Phonemes to graphemes (vowels)

	Correspondences found in many different words		High-frequency words containing rare or unique correspondences (graphemes are underlined)
Phoneme	Grapheme(s)	Sample words	
/a/	a	ant	
/e/	e, ea	egg, head	s<u>ai</u>d, s<u>ay</u>s, fri<u>e</u>nd, l<u>eo</u>pard, <u>a</u>ny
/i/	i, y	in, gym	w<u>o</u>men, b<u>u</u>sy, b<u>ui</u>ld, pr<u>e</u>tty, engin<u>e</u>
/o/	o, a	on, was	
/u/	u, o, o-e	up, son, come	y<u>ou</u>ng, d<u>oe</u>s, bl<u>oo</u>d
/ai/	ai, ay, a-e	rain, day, make	th<u>ey</u>, v<u>ei</u>l, w<u>eigh</u>, str<u>aigh</u>t
/ee/	ee, ea, e, ie	feet, sea, he, chief	th<u>ese</u>[1], p<u>eo</u>ple
/igh/	igh, ie, y, i-e, i	night, tie, my, like, find	h<u>eigh</u>t, <u>eye</u>, <u>I</u>, goodb<u>ye</u>, t<u>ype</u>
/oa/	oa, ow, o, oe, o-e	boat, grow, toe, go, home	<u>oh</u>, th<u>ough</u>, f<u>ol</u>k
/oo/	oo, ew, ue, u-e	boot, grew, blue, rule	t<u>o</u>, s<u>ou</u>p, thr<u>ough</u>, tw<u>o</u>, l<u>o</u>se
/oo/	oo, u	look, put	c<u>ou</u>ld
/ar/	ar, a	farm, father	c<u>al</u>m, <u>are</u>, <u>au</u>nt, h<u>ear</u>t
/or/	or, aw, au, ore, al	for, saw, Paul, more, talk	c<u>augh</u>t, th<u>ough</u>t, f<u>our</u>, d<u>oor</u>, br<u>oa</u>d
/ur/	ur, er, ir, or (after 'w')	hurt, her, girl, work	l<u>ear</u>n, j<u>our</u>ney, w<u>ere</u>
/ow/	ow, ou	cow, out	dr<u>ough</u>t
/oi/	oi, oy	coin, boy	
/air/	air, are, ear	fair, care, bear	th<u>ere</u>
/ear/	ear, eer, ere	dear, deer, here	p<u>ier</u>
/ure/[2]			s<u>ure</u>, p<u>oor</u>, t<u>our</u>
/ə/	many different graphemes	corn<u>er</u>, pill<u>ar</u>, mot<u>or</u>, fam<u>ous</u>, fav<u>our</u>, murm<u>ur</u>, ab<u>ou</u>t, cott<u>on</u>, mount<u>ai</u>n, poss<u>i</u>ble, happ<u>en</u>, cent<u>re</u>, thor<u>ough</u>, pict<u>ure</u>, cupb<u>oar</u>d... and others		

In the last column words printed in italic are from the list of 100 words occurring most frequently in children's books.

[1] The 'e-e' spelling is rare in words of one syllable but is quite common in longer words, (e.g. *grapheme, phoneme, complete, recede, concrete, centipede*).

[2] The pronunciation of the vowel sound in *sure, poor* and *tour* as a diphthong (a short /oo/ sound followed by a schwa) occurs in relatively few words and does not occur in everyone's speech.

Table 3: Graphemes to phonemes (consonants)

	Correspondences found in many different words		Correspondences found in some high-frequency words but not in many/any other words
Grapheme	Phoneme(s)	Sample words	
b, bb	/b/	bat, rabbit	lamb, debt
c	/k/, /s/	cat, cell	special
cc	/k/, /ks/	account, success	
ch	/ch/	chip	school, chef
ck	/k/	duck	
d, dd	/d/	dog, muddy	
dg	/j/	badge	
f, ff	/f/	fan, puff	of
g	/g/, /j/	go, gem	
gg	/g/, /j/	bigger, suggest	
gh	/g/, /-/	ghost, high	rough
gn	/n/	gnat, sign	
gu	/g/		guard
h	/h/	hen	honest
j	/j/	jet	
k	/k/	kit	
kn	/n/	knot	
l	/l/	leg	half
ll	/l/	bell	
le	/l/ or /əl/	paddle	
m, mm	/m/	map, hammer	
mb	/m/		lamb
mn	/m/		autumn
n	/n/, /ng/	net, pink	
nn	/n/	funny	
ng	/ng/, /ng+g/, /n+j/	ring, finger, danger	
p, pp	/p/	pen, happy	
ph	/f/	photo	
qu	/kw/	quiz	mosquito
r, rr	/r/	rat, carrot	
rh	/r/		rhyme
s	/s/, /z/	sun, is	sure, measure

Table 3: continued

ss	/s/, /sh/	miss, mission	
sc	/s/	scent	
se	/s/, /z/	mouse, please	
sh	/sh/	shop	
t, tt	/t/	tap, butter	listen
tch	/ch/	catch	
th	/th/, /th/ thin, then	Thomas	
v	/v/	van	
w	/w/	wig	answer
wh	/w/ or /hw/	when	who
wr	/r/	write	
x	/ks/ /gz/	box, exam	xylophone
y	/y/, /i/ (/ee/), /igh/	yes, gym, very, fly	
ye, y-e			goodbye, type
z, zz	/z/	zip, buzz	

In the last column words printed in italic are from the list of 100 words occurring most frequently in children's books.

Table 4: Graphemes to phonemes (vowels)

	Correspondences found in many different words		Correspondences found in some high-frequency words but not in many/any other words
Grapheme	Phoneme(s)	Sample words	
a	/a/, /o/, /ar/	ant, was, father	water, any
a-e	/ai/	make	
ai	/ai/	rain	*said*
air	/air/	hair	
al, all	/al/, /orl/, /or/	Val, shall, always, all, talk	half
ar	/ar/	farm	war
are	/air/	care	*are*
au	/or/	Paul	aunt
augh			caught, laugh
aw	/or/	saw	
ay	/ai/	say	says
e	/e/, /ee/	egg, he	
ea	/ee/, /e/	bead, head	great
ear	/ear/	hear	learn, heart

Table 4: continued

ed	/d/, /t/, /ed/	turned, jumped, landed	
ee	/ee/	bee	
e-e	/ee/	these	
eer	/ear/	deer	
ei	/ee/	receive	veil, leisure
eigh	/ai/	eight	height
er	/ur/	her	
ere	/ear/	here	*were, there*
eu	/yoo/	Euston	
ew	/yoo/, /oo/	few, flew	sew
ey	/i/ (/ee/)	donkey	*they*
i	/i/, /igh/	in, mind	
ie	/igh/, /ee/, /i/	tie, chief, babies	friend
i-e	/igh/, /i/, /ee/	like, engine, machine	
igh	/igh/	night	
ir	/ur/	girl	
o	/o/, /oa/, /u/	on, go, won	*do*, wolf
oa	/oa/	boat	broad
oe	/oa/	toe	shoe
o-e	/oa/, /u/	home, come	
oi	/oi/	coin	
oo	/oo/, /oo/	boot, look	blood
or	/or/, /ur/	for	work
ou	/ow/, /oo/	out, you	*could*, young, shoulder
our	/owə/, /or/	our, your	journey, tour (see table 2, footnote 2)
ow	/ow/, /oa/	cow, slow	
oy	/oi/	boy	
u	/u/, /oo/	up, put	
ue	/oo/, /yoo/	clue, cue	
u-e	/oo/, /yoo/	rude, cute	
ui			build, fruit
ur	/ur/	fur	
uy			buy

In the last column words printed in italic are from the list of 100 words occurring most frequently in children's books.

To avoid lengthening this table considerably, graphemes for the schwa are not included, but see table 2.

Source: *Letters and Sounds: Principles and Practice of High Quality Phonics, Notes of Guidance for Practitioners and Teachers* (DfES Publications 2007, pages 23–26)

Index

Also available in the English Language Teaching Essentials Series:

Introducing English to Young Children: Spoken Language

by Opal Dunn

ISBN 978-0-00-752255-2

Easy to read and full of practical information, *Introducing English to Young Children: Spoken Language* explains how very young and young children begin to acquire English, suggesting how teachers and parents can 'tune into' young children's developmental needs and support them. The book introduces lesson plans and a wide selection of useful oral activities for 3- to 8-year-olds. It also includes tips for classroom management, projects, games and simple picture books that can be used from the first lessons.

Contents

1 Very young and young children and language learning

2 Fitting the syllabus to the child

7 Introducing picture books

8 Oral projects – holistic activities

9 Culture

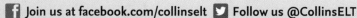

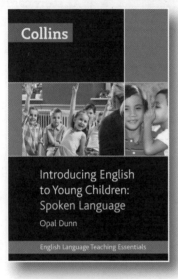
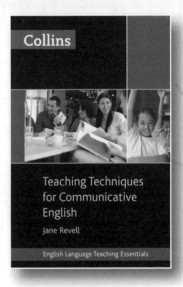